THE
GREEN
GUIDE

For a Sustainable and Profitable Economy in
Hospitality, Retail, and Home Businesses

BRUNO G. KRIOUSSIS

iUniverse, Inc.
Bloomington

The Green Guide
For a Sustainable and Profitable Economy in Hospitality, Retail, and Home Businesses

iUniverse books may be ordered through booksellers or by contacting:

iUniverse
1663 Liberty Drive
Bloomington, IN 47403
www.iuniverse.com
1-800-Authors (1-800-288-4677)

ISBN: 978-1-4620-1003-5 (pbk)
ISBN: 978-1-4620-1004-2 (ebk)

Printed in the United States of America

iUniverse rev. date: 06/18/2011

Contents

Foreword:

Ecology Means Business!

Congratulations on acquiring this copy of *The Green Guide*—simple and practical steps you can take to ensure your business gains the maximum benefits in cost and energy savings.

The information in this guide is invaluable. By implementing these recommendations, you will become a leader in demonstrating the vital necessity of financial stewardship, positively impacting your bottom line while experiencing the satisfaction of preserving our planet.

Our Community in Northern Colorado

It's no accident that the Institute of Ecolonomics (IOE) is headquartered in Fort Collins, Colorado, a community that is passionate about its natural resources and environment. Consistently at the top of the charts among the best places to live, the surrounding area encompasses plains and foothills with a mild climate that accommodates outdoor events in every season. We have a long history of developing and implementing renewable energy, both in private businesses and in the research labs of Colorado State University (CSU). As the largest employer in Fort Collins (the city widely regarded as the regional employment and retail center for Northern Colorado, Southern Wyoming, and Western Nebraska), CSU reflects the high standards that a well-educated community demands.

So many efforts emphasize the relationship between this community and its environment: sustainable living fairs, local farmers' markets, and the armies of volunteers and business persons who strive every day to find sustainable ways to do business. It is this culture that defines Northern Colorado and makes this guide possible. In fact, the Natural Resources Defense Council has listed Fort Collins as one of 22 cities on its 2010 Smarter Cities sustainability list.[1] In a July 19, 2009, article in the *Coloradoan,* Paul McRandle, consulting senior editor of the Smarter Cities Program, noted two IOE efforts as two important contributions to this ranking: the green energy project Fort ZED, and the Climate Wise Program to reduce greenhouse gas emissions.

At the Institute of Ecolonomics, our most important objective is to help you implement the very best business practices for your organization. *The Green Guide* is guaranteed to educate you on, demonstrate to you, and suggest alternatives that you can embrace immediately.

Ecolonomics

Are you familiar with the word *ecolonomics*? This word was created by a good friend of mine—the late actor Dennis Weaver, the founder of IOE. It means 'a healthy relationship that exists between ecology and economics.'[2]

Ecolonomics is a mindset. Once we accept it, we begin to operate with great vigor toward reversing the trend of destroying those things we depend on for sustenance: our irreplaceable natural resources.

As you turn the pages of this book, keep in mind that what you do matters. Increasing the profitability of your company by doing the right thing will change the way those who follow you do business.

I hope you'll join us in working toward a greener way of doing business. I know this guide will take you a long way. Let's work together in becoming more ecolonomic ... because ecology means business!

~ Scott Fardulis, CEO, Institute of Ecolonomics

Preface:

My Green Success Story—and Yours

As you have just read, Ecolonomics is the important merging of business practices that make sense both economically and ecologically. My own green success story began in 2006.

At that time, my wife, Anne, and I decided it was time to make our lives more energy efficient—or pay the financial and environmental consequences. We already lived in a passive solar home (built in 1983) and practiced commonsense energy savings tips, like turning off the lights when we left a room and turning off the water while we brushed our teeth. But we realized we could do much more.

So we invested $5,000 to update our outdated solar water heating system, and we replaced our last few remaining incandescent light bulbs with the most efficient and lowest-wattage light emitting diode (LED) and compact fluorescent (CFL) light bulbs we could find. I spent many hours analyzing the temperatures and airflows of each room and then physically marked each room's thermostat to the ideal temperature. By checking the airflows, I found out that I could lower the thermostats in certain places and still keep the house at an ideal temperature. We spent a little more time and money on recommended maintenance and changed the heads on our old sprinkler system. In total, we spent about $7,000 over a four-year period. No, we didn't pay for everything at once, and yes, we continued to make changes. But the savings we achieved using the principles you will learn in this guide were far beyond what we had considered possible.

In our two-thousand-square-foot home with three bedrooms and two and a half baths, we reduced our spending to an average of $52 a month in energy (we use only electricity) and $25 a month in water and sewer—and we have the utility bills to prove it! In summary, we achieved an energy savings of 71 percent or $2,200 per year,[3] and a water savings of 60 percent or 127,750 gallons per year over the average American family.[4] As for natural gas, we simply don't use it. Factor in our overflowing recycling bins and super-small trash can, and we felt pretty good about our efforts. And we weren't done!

Even more surprising, we discovered that many of the changes were physical improvements that only needed to be done once—one-time expenses. Other huge savings were simply the result of changing our habits—and that's free. I realized that the same type of changes could easily be applied to the workplace. At that time, I owned a restaurant and a home-based business, so my next project was greening them up. That, too, continues to be a success story. Much of what I learned is reflected in this guide. The green techniques in this book will help you save money and save the environment.

My professional position with the Institute of Ecolonomics has provided me with the opportunity to share my achievements there, but my successes with the greening philosophy started at my home in Colorado. My achievements over the last three years are evidence of how, with a little thought and effort, individuals can achieve major energy savings not only in their homes but in their hospitality, retail, or home businesses. And in the process they can positively effect environmental change in their community and beyond. The changes my family and I made in our home and businesses are things you can do, too—starting today, by reading this guide.

Why Go Green?

Why go green? First, it is common sense to want to make the world a better place for ourselves, our children, and our children's children by running businesses that are green and sustainable. **Green** implies protecting people's health and well-being through the use of natural products and safer procedures. **Sustainable** implies reducing the environmental impact from the manufacturer to the product user.

Being both green and sustainable are both great goals for the earth and its creatures. On the more pragmatic side, going green also provides three important benefits to your business and to you as a business owner or entrepreneur:

- **Increased profits.** The money you save by using less electricity, natural gas, and water goes directly to your bottom line.
- **Better quality of operations for your business.** Working toward long-term sustainability decreases your pollutants which can only improve the quality of your operations.
- **Enhanced reputation.** Your reputation will be enhanced—with your customers and within the community.

Even taking small steps toward going green will result in positive gains. Better yet, these goals can be achieved more easily than you think!

Choose a Light Green or Dark Green Approach

Embarking on a greening mission can be overwhelming. So rather than try to do everything at once, we encourage you to think of your improvements as those that are easy to implement right away, on a low (or even no) budget, and those that take a substantial capital investment.

- Light Green **tips** are low-budget, often behavioral changes that can result in significant savings (for example, replacing incandescent bulbs with energy-efficient light bulbs and turning off lights that are not in use).
- **Dark Green tips** may require a larger budget and a more aggressive attitude, though they can yield major savings and generate even more profit (for example, hiring an energy auditor or investing in Energy Star–rated equipment).

In this guide you'll find Light Green **tips** and **Dark Green tips** for virtually every area of your business.

Seven Steps to Greening Your Business and Keeping It Green

The Green Guide is filled with practical techniques you can use right away—seven simple steps for greening your business and keeping the green cycle going:

Step 1: Find a mentor. Getting guidance from someone who's been there is always a good way to start.

Step 2: Gather your Green Team and create a Green Policy. Enlisting the help of your staff puts everyone on the side of sustainability from the beginning.

Step 3: Assess your needs. Find out where to go next by discovering where you are right now.

Step 4: Create your Green Action Plan. Prioritize your needs and decide what needs to be done.

Step 5: Put your Green Action Plan into practice. Start turning your business green!

Step 6: Document your success. Keep track of the money you're saving.

Step 7: Be a mentor. Keep the green cycle going by helping someone else.

As you can see, *The Green Guide* advocates mentoring. Obtaining guidance from those who have walked this path before you, and passing the wisdom on to another business owner when you're ready to do so, is the best way to achieve success and keep the green cycle going. We hope this guide will be your first mentor. Once you've begun, you'll find many opportunities to acquire information that will further help you make your business green. The Internet provides an inexhaustible amount of information; the many online resources at the end of this book barely scratch the surface of what's available. Green fairs, professional speakers, university classes, and simple public awareness seminars add even more.

Ready? Start now!

~ Bruno Gerard Krioussis, VP of Operations, Institute of Ecolonomics

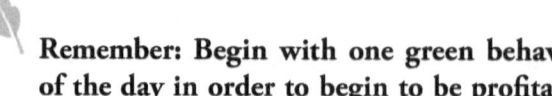

Remember: Begin with one green behavior before the end of the day in order to begin to be profitable and sustainable tomorrow.

Acknowledgments

I would like to extend a personal thank-you to Anne L. Krioussis, Kathy Collier, Marc Wanger, Bevan Suits, Gailmarie Kimmel, Scott Fardulis, Juliette Fardulis, and Mark Coleman for your insight, proofreading, and criticisms. Last but not least, my heartfelt appreciation goes to my lovely wife, Anne, for her unconditional support and patience in helping me with the coherence of this guide.

Your 7-Step Green Business Action Plan

Step 1

Find a Mentor

The decision to transform your business into a green and sustainable concern is an exciting proposition ... but where do you start?

You are probably not a sustainability specialist, and your business may keep you too busy to gain the expertise you need to begin. So it just makes sense to get the advice and guidance of someone who has already been through the process of greening a business. That's why our first step is to encourage you to find and use a mentor who can help you think about what you need to do to green your business.

Mentoring is a structured and trusting relationship that brings business owners, Green Team leaders, and other decision makers together with a caring person (perhaps an initiative volunteer, a private company employee, a local government specialist, or a nonprofit organization member, for instance) who offers guidance, support, encouragement, and practical ideas.

Finding a Mentor

If you already know business owners who have had experience with greening their businesses, ask if they can sit down and talk with you about what they learned or if they can recommend someone who can. Together, you can follow the guidelines in *The Green Guide*.

If you do not already have someone in mind, contact your local chamber of commerce, networking group, or professional business association in your industry and ask about any leaders in the energy efficiency field. You

3

can even search local and regional newspaper databases to find the names of companies that have had articles written about them mentioning energy improvements.

In Fort Collins, Colorado, at least two local organizations will help in making changes to your business—Climate Wise and Fort ZED:

- **Climate Wise** (www.fcgov.com/climatewise). Program Manager and Coordinator Kathy Collier (with the City of the Fort Collins Natural Resources Department) and her Outreach Specialist Team are there for you. The goal of the Climate Wise program is to reduce greenhouse gas emissions by promoting waste reduction, energy savings, alternative transportation, and water conservation and by practicing pollution prevention. The Climate Wise program is helping the Fort Collins community meet some of its greenhouse gas reduction goals as highlighted in the Local Action Plan to Reduce Greenhouse Gas Emissions, which was adopted by the Fort Collins City Council. According to Climate Wise, businesses participating in the program have reduced greenhouse gas emissions by 116,907 tons of CO_2 in 2009. This represents more than 40 percent of Fort Collins's overall reduction.[5] They offer help ranging from do-it-yourself to fully assisted projects in exchange for a full reporting of your results.

- **FortZED** (www.fortzed.com). Coordinator Mark Wanger and his team of volunteers are also available to you at FortZED, which is growing to be the world's largest active zero-energy district. FortZED is a set of active projects and initiatives created by public–private partnerships, and they use Smart Grid and renewable energy technologies to achieve local power generation and energy demand management. Located in downtown Fort Collins, the project is a collaborative effort, sharing best practices at the state, regional, national, and global levels. The FortZED volunteers are ready to jump in and help you make changes and implement projects that you may identify during the assessment phase detailed in Step 2, below.[6]

Get Started!

Even if you choose not to use a mentor, the practical steps outlined in *The Green Guide* will show you what you need to do. By following this process, you can gain firsthand knowledge about greening your business—and, if you choose, you can use that knowledge to mentor someone else in their own projects, the final step in continuing the green cycle.

Step 2

Gather Your Green Team and Create a Green Policy

As the business owner or entrepreneur, you are the ultimate decision maker. But you can't do it alone! It's good practice to involve other people from your organization in any plan that will ultimately affect everyone, such as one to green your business.

Going green and staying green takes teamwork; everyone on your staff needs to understand your goals. If one employee feels free to leave the lights on every night instead of turning them off, this simple, unthinking act will undercut your efforts. Keep everyone informed and help them feel involved. If you obtain a commitment from management in all organizational areas affected by the changes before you finalize them and work with key employees to help communicate your Green Action Plan to the rest of the organization, you will be halfway to success before you even start!

Create a Dedicated Green Team

Your Green Team will help you with your green transformation—but that's not all! They will also help you make your business more sustainable while at the same time making it more profitable.

Gather your team members. No one knows what goes on in your business better than the people who work there every day, so begin by establishing a Green Team of managers and key employees. These will be the people to help you execute green management activities across different parts of your organization, and they will also be key partners in ensuring integration of best practices.

Explain your green vision for the business. Communicate your vision for the organization clearly. It's important that your management team understands the importance of the green changes and makes sustainability part of not just your operations, but also your company culture.

Ask for input. Be sure your key employees are involved in the decision making process and changes. Make them part of the solution by asking for their ideas and participation; they are the ones who will make the greatest impact during the implementation of the changes.

Appoint a team leader. If you run a small business, you can be the team leader. But if you have many other responsibilities and can't oversee everything yourself, appoint a Green Team leader to be responsible for setting goals, tracking progress, and promoting the green management program.

Share your vision with the entire staff. Once you have the support and commitment of your managers and key employees, share your company's new vision with the rest of the staff. You may be surprised to learn that some people already practice green behavior at home and want to do the same at work. If they are very enthusiastic, include them on your Green Team.

Promote ongoing employee engagement. Create a learning environment, taking new ideas from anyone and sharing them with everyone and making decisions as a team rather than from the top down. Then, when a decision has been made, everyone will share the responsibility for doing it.

Create Green Policies

With your Green Team, create policies that spell out the way you will do business in accordance with your green and sustainable philosophy. This goes beyond a vision or mission statement to practical intentions. For example:

- Your business will only buy recycled paper products and will in turn recycle that paper routinely.
- You will do everything possible to buy local goods and sustainably grown products and will pledge to recycle and/or compost waste.
- Lights will be turned off when it is not necessary to keep them on.
- You will walk or bike for business purposes whenever possible, rather than use motor transportation, and will encourage all employees to do so as well.

Of course, once you have assessed your needs and created an action plan, your policies will grow. But simple policies like these will lay the foundation for setting performance goals and integrating green management into your organization's culture and operations every day, on deeper levels.

Record your Green Policies in your operating manual or employee guidelines, give everyone a copy, and make sure they understand it.

Tackle these Steps as a Team

Involve everyone in Step 3 of forming a Green Action Plan, discussed in detail in the next chapter, which is conducting an assessment of your current operations and discovering what you can do to make improvements. Discuss this information so everyone understands what they will be looking for when forming the plan.

Making everyone part of the solution is a great way to ensure compliance as time goes on, so be sure that everyone on the team has input into the steps involved in creating and implementing your Green Action Plan.

Change Is Good!

About three months after the start of your Green Action Plan's implementation, check that everyone is still "talking the talk" and that managers are leading by example. If you are facing some difficulties from some individuals, deal with it from the top. Business owners should discuss and emphasize compliance with management; and management should address compliance with the lower employees.

After this time period, include the new green policies as part of each employee and manager job description, and make it understood that employees will be evaluated on these tasks. If, over time, some individuals are not performing properly with their green tasks, such a performance issue must be dealt with the same as any job performance issue.

Changes made to become green can be behavioral, or technical, or a blend of both. Embarking on a greening mission can be overwhelming, but perhaps by thinking in terms of going from light to dark—from low-budget investments to a substantial capital investment—will help. "Light Green" modifications involve less spending, but with more focus on behavioral factors, which can still save significant costs. Meanwhile, a "**Dark Green**" approach involves larger upfront costs and a more aggressive attitude, though over time it can yield major savings and generate even more profit.

Business owners and employees can sometimes fear changes, be stressed and overloaded with work, not have extra money to spare, have a very limited time frame, or may become confused with too much information. So, delegate. Share ideas, decisions, and responsibilities. Remember that making mistakes is part of the learning experience. Do not instill punishment as part of your policy enforcement system; instead, encourage the trial of new ideas (within an acceptable structure) and systems as part of your policy.

After twenty-nine years of hospitality experience, I have found that most people feel secure when they are familiar with the same old routine. When they need to adapt to a new situation or make changes, I have discovered that roughly one-third of the people are fearful, one-third love the change, and one-third simply follow the majority! So the best strategy in going green is to work first with the people who love making changes and then work with the people who fear the changes ... and the rest will follow!

 Remember: An employee who is not part of the solution is part of the problem! Make everyone on your staff be part of the solution by involving them in the decision making process!

Step 3

Assess Your Needs

I have always taken my businesses seriously, and I'm sure you take your business seriously too. You want to be successful and contribute positively to your community. Becoming sustainable—not merely buying environmentally friendly goods like cleaning products and paper towels, but going green in every dimension—can result in serious contributions to your community and serious savings.

Chances are there are many areas in your business you haven't considered where green changes can help your bottom line. Don't begin by assuming you already know the problems. Begin by gathering data about all of these areas:

- Operations and Behaviors
- Building and Construction
- Consumable Products and Operational Supplies
- Equipment and Appliances
- Utilities: Water, Sewage, and Energy
- Lighting
- Chemicals
- Pollution Prevention and Waste Management
- Landscape and Gardening
- Transportation
- Marketing
- Accounting

The rest of this chapter goes into these areas in more detail. Use the Green Action Plan Checklist as a guide as the items it contains will be discussed extensively. I guarantee that you will discover more areas for change than you ever believed possible!

Green Action Plan Checklist

1. Operations and Behaviors

1.1 Business Type

1.2 Hours of Operation for Staff and Vendors

1.3 Hours of Operation for Customer Service

1.4 Management and Staff

    1.4.1 Behavioral Observations

    1.4.2 Shift Procedures

    1.4.3 Staff Equipment Operations

    1.4.4 Waste Management, Recycling, and Composting

    1.4.5 Transportation

1.5 Vendors and Purchasing

1.6 Service Companies and Other Contractors

1.7 Systems and Procedures in Place

    1.7.1 Company Culture and Policy

    1.7.2 Manual of Operations and Employee Handbook

    1.7.3 Vendor Contracts

    1.7.4 Service Contracts

    1.7.5 Local and Federal Regulations

2. Building and Construction

2.1 Building Structure and Envelope

2.2 Interior Space and Design

2.3 Water and Sewage Systems

1. Operations and Behaviors

First, assess the general operation of your business. You will want to look at the type of business you're in, its general operations, and the behavior of your staff and customers.

1.1 Business Type

What type of business do you operate? This can make a bigger difference than you might realize. For example, a restaurant can use five times more energy per square foot than a clothing store; a clothing store will use most of its energy during the day; and a hotel will use most of its energy to keep the building comfortable for guests 24/7, 365 days a year. In addition, water and energy used for customer showers and washing linen put even more of a burden on hotel utility bills, while other businesses will have other expenses (and therefore, other areas in which to go green).

Clearly it is very important to make a plan that takes into account your kind of business. If you're running a restaurant, you will probably want your first changes to be in reducing energy costs in the kitchen. If you own a hotel, water usage is crucial. If you own a gift shop, you may want to concentrate on products like recycled wrapping paper, creative packaging, and even gift items that help rather than hurt the environment.

1.2 Hours of Operation for Staff and Vendors

What are your real hours of operation, from first deliveries to final closing? Every hour that you are open for business, you are using energy!

Your hours of operation affect your energy use for heat, air-conditioning, lighting, and so on. Most businesses have three different atmosphere settings: one when there are customers inside the building (business mode), a second one when only employees and vendors are present (economic mode), and a third one when the building is totally closed (saving mode). You can think of atmosphere settings as ABC: Ambiance, Behavior, and Comfort.

- **Ambiance** is influenced by lighting, music, and decorations. Lighting and music will directly impact your electric bills.
- **Behavior** is impacted by your management style; genuinely caring about your employees will have the most positive effect.

Make your employees part of the solution, and make decisions *with* your staff rather than *for* them. Informed and committed employees will use your utilities in a way that decreases waste and directly impacts energy bills.

- **Comfort** depends on your temperature and humidity settings, which in turn directly affects your electric and other energy bills.

Light Green **Tips:**

- Turn off lights and music in unoccupied rooms.
- Close vents and doors to unused rooms.
- Use your HVAC according to the season, and be more proactive during the "swing" months with regard to adjusting your settings. Know your climate! Depending on where you live, the swing months can last one-third of the year. This is where your understanding of how to properly use your HVAC will really impact your utility bills. *This is a weekly and monthly behavior to adopt.*
- Avoid using your electrical equipment during coincident peak hours (when the utility company charges the highest rate due to the highest demand). Schedule your use wisely and in accordance with your staffing. Review and check with employees daily in order to emphasize the importance of using electricity at off-peak hours. *This is a daily behavior to adopt.*

Dark Green Tip:

- Install a programmable thermostat in every room to maintain the appropriate and most cost effective temperature setting.

1.3 Hours of Operation for Customer Service

What hours are your business open to customers? During the hours when customers are in your building, you want their experience to be pleasant—which means you will have to focus more on lighting and appropriate temperature.

By using high-quality, energy-efficient lighting, you can maintain or improve your business's ambiance and save energy at the same time! You win on both sides: higher quality and less money.

Light Green **Tips:**

- Have two settings for lighting and music: one for when your business is open and one for when it is closed, but you still have employees inside the building.

Dark Green Tip:

- If your business is open 24/7, like a hotel, invest in Energy Star–rated equipment and energy-efficient lighting. This investment will pay off, in energy savings, immediately.

1.4 Management and Staff

Do your employees understand how they can do their work in a greener way? Your staff and managers can have a major impact on the money you spend on energy.

For example, in one restaurant I owned, I noticed a huge peak of kilowatt usage every day around 6 a.m. I soon discovered that my cleaning crew was routinely turning on all the lights inside the building—including the decorative ones. It was a holiday party every day! So, I explained my energy savings plan, and invited them to be part of the solution. I asked them to select only the lights that they really needed to perform the job. Then, with an 89-cent black permanent marker, we marked those dimmers "CC," for cleaning crew. From then on those were the only lights the crew turned on to conduct their work. At the end of the next month, my bill showed that energy use for lighting to clean the entire building had been slashed to one-third its previous level—and all at the cost of a black marker!

1.0.1 Behavioral Observations: Spend some time observing and taking notes about the habits of *all* the people using the building—employees, vendors, and service providers—before you jump to conclusions about their behavior and how it effects the usage of energy. You may be surprised!

Light Green **Tips:**

- Buy fleece vests for employees who open the business so they can keep thermostats turned down until heat is needed.
- Keep the thermostat low for the cleaning crew.

- For restaurants, defrost frozen food in the fridge two to three days in advance rather than thawing under running water for hours. The energy used to thaw the product will be greatly reduced, you won't waste water, and it's better for food safety. To do this without disruption to your business, make sure the kitchen manager maintains a list of frozen foods to pull into the refrigerator for thawing. Review usage of products daily and check the kitchen staff to ensure compliance.

Dark Green Tips:

- Make sure your Green Team is always part of the solution. If staff members are not following the company's Green Policy, explain how important it is for them to do so. Give them a chance to correct their behavior; some people will need more time than others to understand and change long-term habits.
- If an employee intentionally breaks the policy, this is an operational issue. You are in charge. Enforce your Green Policy just as you do your other company policies.

1.4.2 Shift Procedures: If your business has just a few employees, shifts will not be an issue. But if your business has a large staff (and in my experience, staffing can comprise one-third of the budget or more), wise scheduling can go a long way to greening your bottom line.

In general, the coincident peak (time of day demand is the highest) of electricity for most establishments is between 3:00 p.m. and 6:00 p.m. during the summer as this is when the temperature dictates that air conditioning usage is the highest.[7] Regardless of exactly how much equipment and electricity your business uses during these peak hours, the cost during that time will form a large percentage of your energy bill. Your utilities provider charges more for electricity used during your coincident peak. Contact them to find out when this is for your area. Then, if you schedule your employees properly, you can impact this cost.

For example, a medium-sized restaurant that is open to the public after 4:00 p.m. will require a group of prep cooks and line cooks to prepare and cook the food for the customers. The food must be prepped before 4:00 p.m., but it's vastly preferable not to use heavy-duty electric prep equipment once peak hours start, around 3:00 p.m. Say the prep cooks need to work about six hours per shift. The solution? Schedule them to arrive at 9:00 a.m.! They will use all the heavy equipment before peak hours. To be even more cost effective, keep all unnecessary HVAC and lighting turned off, even in the kitchen, until 3:30 p.m., when the main staff arrives to get the dining room ready to open.

Light Green Tips:

- Write a schedule that puts properly trained and educated employees at the right place at the right time.
- Schedule deliveries during off-peak hours so employees are not opening outside doors or walking in and out of freezers and walk-ins when electricity is most expensive.

Dark Green Tip:

- Invest in computer software appropriate for your industry to help manage your manpower.

1.4.3 Staff Equipment Operations: Staffing and equipment usage work together to affect your electricity usage and cost. Distributing your equipment usage to off-peak hours will also have a very significant impact. Even small daily savings add up to a lot over the course of a year.

Light Green Tip:

- Modify some settings on your electrical equipment. For example, reprogram the defrost time for your fridges and freezers to defrost between 4:00 p.m. and 6:00 p.m., when the coincident peak demand is at its highest.

Dark Green Tip:

- Invest in new timers and other electrical devices to monitor your equipment. Consult your preventive maintenance company for recommendations.

1.4.4 Waste Management, Recycling, and Composting: Municipal services in most areas of the United States are equipped to help you with waste management, recycling, and composting. But first you have to help yourself. Before you throw anything away, think. And have your employees do the same!

Tips:

- Analyze your operational needs and make decisions on which services to utilize based on your local city programs.
- If you have a garden, consider putting your organic waste in a compost pile, which later you can use to fertilize your plants.
- If you run a restaurant or provide food services, try to use every scrap of the meat and produce you buy. Be creative in your menu! Most restaurant owners already know that throwing away vegetable peels that could go into a stock is throwing away money.

1.4.5 Transportation: Petroleum fuels contribute to pollution, and gas-powered vehicles cost more and more money to operate as fuel prices generally trend upward with time. Here is a place where you can really save some money by making a few small behavioral changes.

Tips:

- Buy local products whenever available. Doing so reduces transportation costs.
- Consolidate your food and supply delivery trips in order to reduce the number of shipments.
- Whenever possible, carpool, walk or use a bicycle.

Dark Green Tip:

- If you are running a small business and use your own transport to run errands, get a hybrid vehicle and consolidate your trips (to the store, to meet clients, and so on).

1.5 Vendors and Purchasing

You may be able to buy certain products that are produced in foreign countries or distant states more cheaply, but green, sustainable practices favor local vendors and local, organic, and seasonal products. By buying local, you can contribute to your community rather than contributing to health and financial costs associated with shipping over long distances and using chemicals to grow food. And once you begin making relationships with local vendors, you may in fact find that the items you buy actually cost the same or less than buying from over a distance.

Light Green **Tips:**

- Purchase local, organic, and seasonal products.
- Purchase reusable and durable products.
- Purchase items in bulk.
- Purchase recycled products.
- Use paper products that contain post-consumer recycled content.
- Consolidate your orders and deliveries.

Dark Green Tip:

- Purchase CO2 offset credits. Consult your Chamber of Commerce for companies that offer this option.

 Remember: Use local, organic, and seasonal goods!

1.6 Service Companies and Other Contractors

Whenever possible, use local service companies. Categories could include anything from carpet cleaning to HVAC maintenance. They will drive a shorter distance and reach you within a shorter amount of time. Unnecessary travel is not green!

Light Green **Tip:**

- Consolidate the work that needs to be done so your service company can do everything in only one visit.

1.7 Systems and Procedures in Place

Are the systems and procedures that you have in place serving your green, sustainable goals? With your Green Team, take a close look at the way you currently do business and look for ways to improve.

1.7.1 Company Culture and Policy: You should already have your Green Policies in place. See if there are any areas you missed and commit to continuing improvement. Organizations that see financial returns from superior energy management are motivated to further improve their energy performance. Their success is based on regularly assessing energy use and implementing steps to increase energy efficiency even more.

Light Green **Tips:**

- Have your green policies in place.
- Involve your management team in the discussion of policies and green decisions.
- Train your staff in green techniques.

Dark Green Tip:

- Hire new people, if needed, and train them according to your Green Policies.

Remember: No matter the size or type of organization, the common element of successful energy management is commitment. Inspect what you expect!

1.7.2 Manual of Operation and Employee Handbook: Do you have a manual of operations and an employee handbook, or do you just expect employees to know what to do? If you already have these documents, you may need to amend them to reflect your new Green Policy. If you don't have them, work with your Green Team to write them, and then make sure all employees have a copy. If you have an employee Intranet, put the documents there, too.

Light Green **Tips:**

- Create checklists to help guide employees (lights turned off/ on, recycling days, etc.).
- Post clear signs that make it easy for staff to remember what needs to be done.
- Post achievements and progress and reward employees in order to encourage everyone to stay on the green track.

Dark Green Tips:

- Write and publish a manual of operations that expresses your Green Policy in concrete terms. Be specific.
- Write an employee handbook—with the assistance of an attorney, if needed.

Remember: The only constant is change. Be constant with it!

1.7.3 Vendor Contracts: Choose vendors that share your green values. If you feel your vendors could be doing more to be green, share your vision, outline what you are looking for, and write down those expectations. Make it a contract and see what happens!

Light Green **Tips:**

- Share your expectations in terms of your green values with your vendors.
- Put your expectations in writing to avoid misunderstandings.

Dark Green Tip:

- Write legal contracts with your vendors regarding green practices.

Remember: A document speaks by itself!

1.7.4 Service Contracts: Buildings and equipment that are kept in good condition will always save you from bad surprises. A preventive maintenance program and a proper contract with a professional maintenance company will always save you money in the long run.

Remember: You can budget for your preventive maintenance costs, but you cannot predict when (or how much) you'll have to pay for a breakdown!

Light Green **Tips:**

- Check the air-conditioning units periodically during the warm months.
- Have a preventive maintenance plan in place for all of your equipment.

Dark Green Tip:

- Have an external company perform a full inspection of your equipment and give you recommendations on maintenance and energy efficient upgrades.

Remember: Preventive maintenance is cheaper than paying for a disaster!

1.7.5 Local and Federal Regulations: The Resource Conservation and Recovery Act (RCRA) is a national public law that creates the framework for the proper management of hazardous and nonhazardous solid waste.[8] Every business must be aware of these laws. Ignorance is not a defense. To become familiar with the parts of RCRA that pertain to your industry, see the Resource Conservation and Recovery Act on line.

Light Green **Tips:**

- Call your local Department of Utilities and/or Department of Water and Power in order to get specific information about your local rules and regulations, as well as on helpful programs for compliance and going green.

Dark Green Tip:

- Consult an attorney specializing in environmental issues if you have specific questions regarding the RCRA.

2. Building and Construction

Your building is your customer's first impression of your business. Thoroughly assess your building's environmental soundness. If you have major issues, you have to be aware of them before you can fix them.

2.1 Building Structure and Envelope

Focus on the big picture first when it comes to your building. Follow the Leadership in Energy & Environmental Design (LEED) rated renovations specifications for old buildings and the LEED-rated new building specifications for new ones. Specifics on this information can be found through the U.S. Green Building Council at www.usgbc.org.

Light Green **Tips:**

- Check your rooftop, gutters, the underside of the roof, and ceilings four times a year for any signs of damage or leaks.
- Have good seals around all your exterior doors and windows.
- Check all your doors and windows four times a year for ill fitting seals and damage.

Dark Green Tips:

- Have a complete building audit performed by a professional LEED-certified company.
- Have your building's walls, ceilings, windows, and floor insulated.
- Weatherize your entire building.

2.2 Interior Space and Design

The inside of your space must balance efficiency, safety, and style. Everything is important, and nothing can be left out—even air. Air must move, and buildings really do breathe. Air carries heat, cold, and moisture, and air that escapes pulls more air in. Determine where air is coming in and flowing out; air must be channeled, not just allowed to seep into and out of cracks.

Remember: Buildings breathe! Ventilation is just as important as heating and cooling.

Light Green **Tips:**

- Check the inside lights on a daily basis for burnt out bulbs (this should be part of management's daily walk through).
- For businesses that utilize walk-in freezers and refrigerators, install NSF-certified air curtains on the walk-in doors. All businesses should consider installing them on high traffic back doors.
- Check and understand the convection of air inside your building.

Dark Green Tip:

- Have a complete building audit performed by a professional company in order to spot ways of improving energy efficiency (such as by sealing drafty doors or windows).

1.3 Water and Sewage Systems

Are you wasting water? There is a high chance that you are. Check your water usage for the past year, and contact your local water company for assistance in spotting inefficiency and recommendations for eliminating it. But don't stop there.

Water and sewage are linked. A full audit by an outside company—*not* your current service company—is of key importance. They will see what you do not, and they will tell you what your current company is not telling you.

Light Green **Tip:**

- Make sure your employees always turn off water when it is not in use.

Dark Green Tips:

- Have a complete building audit performed by a professional plumbing company, a grease interceptor service company, and/ or a landscaping company, as applicable to your industry. This will give you a good idea where you are wasting water and what you can do about it.

Remember: Every drop counts!

2.4 HVAC System

Heating, ventilation, and air-conditioning (HVAC) is a complex area that involves many service components, including water, energy, and equipment maintenance. A thorough understanding of the system is extremely important if you wish to make significant improvements in this area. Many HVAC companies are creating new products and more efficient equipment, and companies that have been manufacturing equipment for commercial use are now making new equipment for residential use. This means every business owner has plenty of options when it comes to HVAC service and equipment.

All of the recommendations in this section are very effective for Northern Colorado, and many of them are useful no matter where your business is located. However, before you make any decision or new investment, make a thorough study of the climate in your area. For example, Northern Colorado has three summer months, five winter months, and four swing months; Alaska has two summer months and ten winter months; and Florida has nine summer months, two swing months, and one winter month. Each area requires very different HVAC considerations.

Light Green **Tips:**

- Keep the building closed tight during the day. At night, ventilate the building naturally (using the natural convection pattern inside the building) or with fans, whenever feasible.
- Clean or replace the furnace filter every month.
- Keep vents clean and clear of furniture.
- Close vents and doors to unused rooms.
- Close fireplace dampers when not in use.
- Remove window-mounted air-conditioners each fall and seal up the opening.
- When current fixtures wear out, replace them with water-conserving ones.

- Install an indoor/outdoor thermometer. Make notes to open windows and/or turn on the exhaust system when the outside temperature is below 70°F (below 21°C).
- Install an electric, high-efficiency ceiling exhaust fan to remove the excess hot air in the top part of your building. These fans save both energy and money when used to maintain a comfortable temperature in your building instead of relying on your air-conditioner all the time.
- Consider an evaporative cooler instead of an air-conditioner if you're based in a dry climate, as it uses about one-quarter of the energy to operate.

Sustainability in Action

Set Your Thermostats According to the Season!

Recalibrate all thermostats according to the season and the outside temperature.

For a living space:

- During summer conditions, in the daytime, set your air-conditioning to 75–78°F (24–26°C)
- During summer conditions, in the nighttime, use vents only if the outside temperature is below 70°F (21°C)
- During winter conditions, in the daytime, set your heater to 60–68°F (16–20°C). If you feel chilly, wear a fleece vest. As a final option, set the thermostat to 68°F in September, 66°F in October, 64°F in November, 62°F in December, and 60°F in January, and keep it at 60°F until the end of the winter season.
- During winter conditions, in the nighttime, set your heater to 60°F (16°C).

For spare bedrooms:

- During summer conditions, set your air-conditioning to 80°F (27°C)
- During winter conditions, set your heating to 50°F (9°C)

For dry food storage areas:

- During summer conditions, set your air-conditioning to 60–70°F (16–21°C)
- During winter conditions, set your heating to 50–60°F (9–16°C)

Dark Green Tips:

- Insulate air ducts that run through unheated basements, crawl spaces and attics.
- Replace water-cooled refrigeration units with air-cooled units.
- Buy a hybrid air-conditioner. It reduces greenhouse gas emissions and can use up to 90 percent less electricity during coincident peak hours (available from Coolerado, Ice-Energy, and other sources).
- If you have inefficient linen-washing equipment, switch to high-efficiency energy and water washer equipment or outsource with a reliable and cost-effective vendor.
- Install a thermal solar system for heating your hot water (you may want extra storage tanks if your business is a restaurant or a hotel).
- Install a photovoltaic (PV) solar energy system to produce your own electricity.
- Use other renewable sources of energy (wind, geothermal, and so on), depending on your location and natural resources.

3. Consumable Products and Operational Supplies

Consumables generally relate to the restaurant business, although other types of businesses may also serve food items on a smaller scale. And even if you only provide coffee and tea and light refreshments for customers, you need to consider cups, plates, utensils, and napkins.

3.1 Concept and Menu Design

One day, my wife stopped at a local farmers' market to buy corn on the cob. She was surprised when the cashier told her the price was $5 for eight ears. She knew that the supermarket across town was selling corn for $1 for six ears. However, she also knew that corn had been shipped in from two hundred miles away in refrigerated trucks. So she proceeded to bargain the farmer's price down to $3 for the eight ears.

Why? First, she really wanted to buy a fresh product (harvested that day from just twenty miles away). Second, it would take gas and time for her to drive to the supermarket later that day for the less expensive corn. Third, she wanted to buy the fresh, local corn because it was a quality product that would taste better, but she had limited funds. By knowing the market price and weighing her options, she made the best choice in terms of value and quality that her budget that day would allow.

We can no longer take the easy road, purchasing and consuming products that originate anywhere in the world. Today, consumers are looking for price, freshness, healthfulness, community, locally produced or seasonal products, and organic goods. People who run restaurants have to be aware of the balance involved in designing and supplying a menu that works sustainably and economically. This probably means changing some purchasing patterns.

Concept and menu design that consciously work *with* the environment are the future of the restaurant industry. These decisions will be even more crucial in the near future as increases in fuel costs for transportation will make exotic and long-distance-shipped fresh food more and more expensive. Additionally, as diners become increasingly educated about sustainability, they become more concerned about the quality of the food they eat and the value of consuming more locally grown products. And you should be concerned about that, too.

The choices you make in menu creation and food selection involve a number of issues:

- **Sourcing**: Your products may be local, shipped in from out of state, or produced in other countries and flown in.
- **Fuel costs:** Where your products come from directly impacts fuel use and costs.
- **Energy efficiency:** The way your menu choices are prepared directly affects your energy use.

A restaurant menu that has been designed a few hundred miles from your business by a research and design team and a marketing executive, using national deals for food, is no longer the best way to go about business. We need to do all that we can to design our menus around local, seasonal products.

Fortunately, there are many ways to accomplish this goal:

- Your menu can be designed by season multiple times a year to capitalize on what foods are available nearby so that local, fresh ingredients can be used as specials or featured dishes.
- Your menu can have a year-round core of dishes, and in each category (soup, salad, entrée, side, vegetable du jour, dessert), a dish can be made with a local product and be advertised as such.
- You can create a smaller menu that changes weekly, using priority local products.

The entire menu does not have to be of local origin. You can always complete a dish with out-of-area products if necessary. The point is to design around local from the beginning.

This type of menu can be very cost effective in terms of ingredients, and it also affects the energy used to process, package, and ship food. Local, fresh products do not require using a large freezer to store frozen food purchased from a national distributor, which saves on electricity. The final steps, of course, are to adapt your cooking techniques and use energy-efficient cooking equipment, which is becoming widely available.

Sustainability in Action

The Value of Creating a Local, Seasonal, Sustainable Menu

The restaurant owner can:

- Decrease the cost of food, packaging, transportation, and marketing.
- Lower the use of energy for storage and cooking.

The consumer gets:

- More value for a meal.
- Healthier food.

- Attractive choices, because the menu changes more frequently.
- The satisfaction of consuming more local products, which are part of the local community.

Light Green **Tip:**

- Buy more local and seasonal products.

Dark Green Tips:

- Redesign your menu to use more local, seasonal products.
- Revise your cooking techniques to use less energy.
- Buy new energy-efficient kitchen equipment.

3.2 Local, Organic, and Sustainable Sources

Organizations that practice *sustainable purchasing* buy goods and services while taking into account not only the economic value (price, quality, availability, functionality), but also the environmental, social, and ethical impacts of the goods and services they purchase at local, regional, and global levels. Sustainable purchasing gives preference to suppliers that generate positive social and environmental outcomes, and it integrates sustainability considerations into product selection so that impacts on society and the environment are minimized throughout the full life cycle of the product.

Sustainable purchasing entails looking at what products are made of, where the raw materials come from, the energy used and emissions "footprint" associated with the products during the manufacturing process, how long the products will last, who has made them and under what working conditions, how they will be ultimately disposed of … and whether the purchase needs to be made at all. Sustainability considers environmental, social, and ethical dimensions and brings benefit to the environment as well as not just the local, but also the regional and global communities.

Buying food grown locally saves fuel. According to a well known study from the Leopold Center for Sustainable Agriculture, "In 1998, the Truck Weighted Average Source Distance (WASD) for the continental United

States was 1,518 miles. A food mile is the distance food travels from where it is grown or raised to where it is ultimately purchased by the consumer or end-user. A WASD can be used to calculate a single distance figure that combines information on the distances from producers to consumers and amount of food product transported."[9] (For more on WASD, see http://www.leopold.iastate.edu/pubs/staff/ppp/.)

Sustainability in Action

Know About the Food You Serve Customers, and Let Them Know, Too

More and more consumers are looking for products that are organic and sustainable. It's important to know where your food comes from and to pass that information along.

Whether you use a local supplier or a national one, you should be informed about food advisories, recalls, and warnings. For instance, Colorado's mountain lakes should be pristine. Yet in August 2009, a "fish consumption advisory" was issued on walleye caught in Horsetooth and Carter Reservoirs in Northern Colorado.[10] Apparently, mercury and other chemicals from coal burning pollute the air and later settle out into lakes high in the mountains during upslope weather events in the Front Range. That mercury then accumulates in the food that you might eat, such as walleye from those reservoirs.

If you need to take an item off the menu for an environmental reason, let your customers know why it is gone. They will also appreciate information about where the vegetables you serve were grown, where your fish were raised and how they were caught, where your meat was raised, and so forth.

Light Green **Tips:**

- Research and develop a menu designed to use mainly Community Supported Agriculture (CSA) farm-grown produce.

- Research and develop a sustainable inventory of consumable products that are locally grown, organic, fair-trade, USDA-approved, cage-free, hormone-free, and so on.
- Create a dynamic menu that uses these products and suits all diet requirements customers may have.
- Do a truck WASD of all products you use, and set a goal of reducing that number every year.
- Track food advisories daily.

Dark Green Tips:

- Buy organic products. They can sometimes be more expensive, but once more people start doing so in the future, they will become less expensive.
- Research local suppliers and use them for your goods in order to further decrease transportation costs.

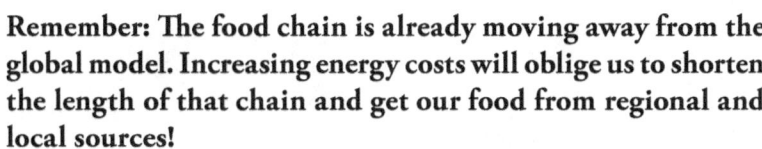

Remember: The food chain is already moving away from the global model. Increasing energy costs will oblige us to shorten the length of that chain and get our food from regional and local sources!

3.3 Disposable Products

Disposable products like cups and utensils are an easy place to begin reducing waste. A wide variety of biodegradable and ecologically sound new products are now available, depending on your business, your needs, and your budget. This is an area where you can make huge improvements. Those improvements may not be immediately visible or significant, but costing per item, per unit, per usage, and per customer will help you to see the impact.

Inform your customers that you have switched to using greener products. They will appreciate it, and it's a very good advertising tool for attracting more green-educated and environmentally conscious consumers.

Light Green **Tip:**

- Try compostable products, and for everything else, recycle, recycle, recycle!

Dark Green Tip:

- Invest in a large order of green product supplies. In the long term, doing so will reduce costs, and use of green products is marketable to environmentally conscious people.

Remember: Your image is also on a disposable beverage cup in a customer's mind!

4. Equipment and Appliances

Businesses use technology of all sorts, including software management tools, systems dealing with data processing, point-of-sale, communication, and security. Many office costs have switched from labor costs to new equipment and electricity costs, along with costs from requiring more skillful managers and staff to operate them.

4.1 Computer and Office

Technology—from software management tools to data processing, communication, security, and point-of-sale systems—is everywhere in the hospitality businesses. Make sure you're not using more systems than you need, use the most energy-efficient technology and equipment possible, and make sure your staff is well trained.

Light Green **Tips:**

- Switch from paper-based office management of data to a digitally-based management philosophy.
- Use smaller scale high energy efficiency desk and task lighting instead of large overhead lighting.
- Save information digitally instead of making paper copies (whenever legally appropriate) to save storage space, money, and trees.
- Contact a local lighting center for further recommendations.

Dark Green Tips:

- Update your office lighting to the most energy efficient *fixtures* possible.
- Buy a fireproof safe for legal documents only, and store information on two external hard drives. Keep one drive in the safe at night and keep one connected to your computer system.

4.2 Entertainment: Music and TV

In the hospitality and retail industries, entertainment is one component of the product sold to the customers. This is part of the green equation because there are significant energy costs associated with entertainment. Doing things in a greener manner and making a few financial investments can greatly affect the costs of using them.

Light Green **Tip:**

- Use your music, TV, and other entertainment systems *only* for customers, not for employees.

Dark Green Tip:

- Update your decorative lighting and your music and TV equipment to the most energy efficient equipment possible.

4.3 Kitchen: Refrigeration and Cooking

In restaurants and bars, the kitchen is the backbone of the business. If your profit comes from food, that food needs to be processed with equipment that involves not only a capital investment, but water, electricity, natural gas, and in some cases other sources of energy. Spare parts and repair and maintenance come into the balance, as well.

Light Green **Tips:**

- Remove frozen items from the blast chiller immediately and turn it off. Blast chillers are one of the largest consumers of electricity in the building!
- Use as few stove burners as possible, especially during slower business hours.

- Turn on only half the grill in the early and late parts of the shift.
- Turn off ovens and fryers when not needed.
- Once a month, check the hot water heater for leaks, temperature calibration, and so on.
- Set your water heater between 120°F minimum and 140°F maximum.

Dark Green Tip:

- Replace your single-pass cooling system with air-cooled options, or install a closed-loop system that recycles cooling water.

4.4 Cleaning and Laundry

Depending on the type of business you operate, this cost can be minimal (someone to clean the office) or a huge part of your operating costs (hotels, restaurants, spas, hair salons, and so on). In restaurants, hotels, and other hospitality businesses, cleaning dishware, flatware, glassware, cookware, and linen is extremely important.

4.4.1 Dishes: If the volume of your food and beverage sales justifies it, lease a dishwashing machine. Let professionals own the care, maintenance, repair, and training of the staff using this piece of equipment. Maintaining an old dish machine is very expensive, and the effectiveness of such a machine is often very low compared to newer machines. It can be a headache to keep it working properly.

Based on my extensive monitoring and tracking of energy usage, I have found that the most effective dish machine is a low-temperature one with no booster. It should be monitored, however, by a professional to ensure that it meets efficiency and health code requirements.

If your business is too small to afford to lease and absorb the cost of a professional dish machine, purchase two small Energy Star–rated machines. Use one for glasses, with a short washing cycle, and one for plates and silverware, using the appropriate cycles. Wash large cooking pots by hand, ideally using a three-compartment sink. The installation of the chemical lines and dispensers for this kind of sink can be done free of charge by a professional from a cleaning product company.

Light Green **Tips:**

- Scrape or brush dishes rather than pre-rinse with water.
- Replace pre-rinse sprayers with water-saving 1.6 gallon per minute sprayers.
- Run full racks rather than partially full racks.
- Turn the dishwasher off when not in use (or use the automatic shut-off device).
- Pre-soak pots and pans in basins or sinks rather than rinsing them in running water.
- Use green cleaning products like Apex from Ecolab or Green Solutions, Biorenewables, and the like to maintain cleanliness without damaging the environment.
- Lease a low-temperature dish machine. You do not want to own maintenance costs, spare parts replacement, and other repair costs. For instance, Ecolab's Apex Warewashing System offers that equipment at a very accessible price.
- Have the dish machine checked once a month (this scheduled maintenance is already included in the Apex program from Ecolab).

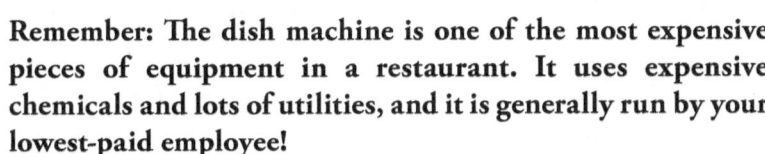

Remember: The dish machine is one of the most expensive pieces of equipment in a restaurant. It uses expensive chemicals and lots of utilities, and it is generally run by your lowest-paid employee!

The dishwashing machine is one of the most interesting and complex pieces of equipment, and it's important to understand all of its implications:

- It uses all of your utilities as a component of your utility bill: hot water (with water and heat—generally natural gas), electricity to run the motor, and sewage.
- It uses at least three different chemicals for the cleaning process (detergent, rinse, and sanitizer).
- It uses specific utensils (spatula scraper, sponge scrubber, squeegee, and a high-pressure sprayer).
- It uses labor to operate it, and the staff member requires a proper uniform: apron and rubber gloves.

- It costs money for repairs, spare parts, and maintenance to keep it in good working condition.
- It costs money to lease it or own it, whichever choice you make.

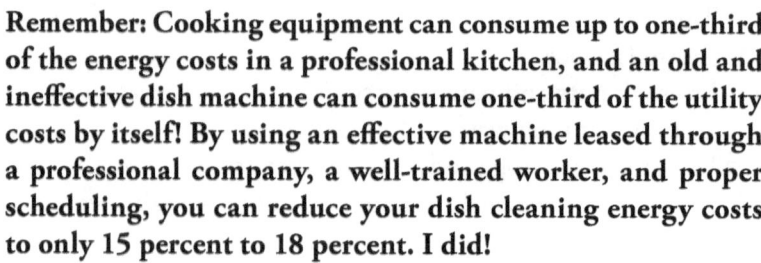

Remember: Cooking equipment can consume up to one-third of the energy costs in a professional kitchen, and an old and ineffective dish machine can consume one-third of the utility costs by itself! By using an effective machine leased through a professional company, a well-trained worker, and proper scheduling, you can reduce your dish cleaning energy costs to only 15 percent to 18 percent. I did!

Dark Green Tip:

- If you want to own your dish machine, buy a new and efficient one, and sell it after five years.

4.4.2 Laundry: Use Energy Star–rated laundry equipment and keep it well maintained and clean, or use a reputable linen service company. As a manager, you need to monitor proper linen usage. Keep these points in mind:

- Make sure employees use the appropriate linen for each job (cleaning towels, napkins, bed linens, etc.).
- Count each type of linen used per shift to set your pars.
- Monitor the gathering of dirty linens so that you and your vendor are on the same page in terms of quantity. Don't let them "rent" you more than you need!

Light Green Tips:

- Separate linen by types, and wash and dry similar types together.
- Wash a full load every time.
- Wash laundry in cold water whenever possible.
- Line-dry linens whenever possible.

- If you use a drying machine, dry two or more loads in a row to take advantage of the heat that remains in the dryer from the first load.
- Know your linen usage.

Dark Green Tip:

- Buy and use Energy Star–rated equipment.

5. Utilities: Water, Sewage, and Energy

When it comes to utilities, the most important consideration is your usage—*not* how much the bill is. This information is easy to find and easy to track.

First, gather your utility bills for the past twelve months and transfer the usage information (kWh, mmbtu, gallons, and so on) to a monthly utility-tracking chart. You can also track the dollar amount, but the main parameter for measuring success at becoming greener is usage. These usage numbers will be your baselines. Right away, you'll see some trends, especially concerning seasons and times of day. If you haven't been paying much attention to these numbers, you may be surprised. Keep track of your usage each month. If you are already applying some light green tactics, you may see the numbers go down right away.

You can use this information to:

- Compare your utility usage with your peers, competitors, or industry standards.
- Understand your usage patterns and trends.
- Determine where you are doing well in terms of green or sustainable usage and where there is room for improvement.

If needed, ask your utility providers to help you interpret your bills in terms of usage, billing method, fixed charges, and variable charges. In my experience, commercial utility bills are much more complicated than residential utility bills, and a full understanding will be of great benefit.

Remember: Because you cannot control the pricing, you must control the usage.

5.1 Water

Our nation's growing population is putting stress on our available water supplies. Over the latter half of the twentieth century, the United States' population nearly doubled, according to data obtained through the U.S. Census Bureau.[11] In that same period, public demand for water more than tripled! According to the EPA, an average American family of four can use 400 gallons of water per day.[12] This increased demand has put additional stress on water supplies and distribution systems, threatening our health and the environment.

Recent government surveys showed that at least two-thirds of the states anticipate local, regional, or statewide shortages by 2013.[13] By using water more efficiently, we can save money, help preserve water supplies, and protect the environment.

Saving water is also saving energy and chemicals. Electricity is needed to supply and treat cold water. In 2008, American public water supply and treatment facilities consumed about 56 billion kilowatt-hours of power.[14] They also continue to use harmful agents like alum, coagulants, and flocculants, and filter aids like sand, gravel, charcoal, polymer, chlorine, fluoride, soda ash, and on and on.

In the near future, communities that focus on conserving water will not need to pay as much to develop new supplies and expand or upgrade water and wastewater infrastructures. Why? Because communities that choose to make improvements while costs are relatively low, will benefit in the future after a crisis or unforeseen increase has occurred.

 Remember: Saving water is saving energy. Letting your faucet run for five minutes uses about as much total energy as leaving on a 60-watt light bulb for 14 hours![15]

Light Green **Tips:**

- Educate all employees about water conservation and involve them in finding ways to save water, and put them into your action plan.

- Place signs in the kitchen and bathrooms promoting water conservation.
- Repair leaks and malfunctioning equipment promptly.
- Check and unclog your drains every day.
- Use low-flow showerheads and faucets.
- Use any water commercial rebates that might be available in your area.
- Use Water Sense–labeled products.
- Thaw food overnight in the refrigerator rather than leaving it in the sink under running water.

Dark Green Tips:

- Replace water-cooled refrigeration units with air-cooled units.
- Replace old icemakers with a new air-cooled, water-efficient model (the useful life of an icemaker is about five years).
- Use softened water in ice cube machines to minimize bleed-off.
- Install low-flow toilets and faucet aerators in restrooms.
- Install hands-free or foot-activated valves or faucets.
- Install sub-meters for multiple users of water.
- Obtain a professional water audit to help identify areas where you can improve conservation.

Remember: With hot water you get hit by utilities three times—once for the water, a second time for the energy to heat it up, and third for the sewer!

5.2 Sewage

Even the most scrupulously clean businesses use water for cleaning and mopping. A good rule of thumb is to prevent anything (even vaguely solid) from clogging a sink or floor drain. Restaurants and food-related businesses, especially, use a lot of water for cleaning pots and pans that have been in contact with fats and oils and mixing bowls that have been used for processing oily dressings. Plus, floors inevitably collect food debris and other waste products, and need to be mopped. This very dirty, oily, and greasy sludge goes directly into the sewage system and clogs your drains, pipes, and grease interceptors.

For every gallon of wastewater sent down the drain to the treatment plant, it takes three (or more) gallons of additional clean water to remove enough debris and toxins to return the dirty portion to safe levels of cleanliness.[16] Installing drain screens in sinks and floor drains means that much of this debris can be thrown into the trash rather than into the grease interceptor or downstream.

Going deeper, you can hire a professional company that specializes in grease interceptors. You can also use products like SCD's Bio Klean products, which are concentrated, all-natural industrial cleaners containing powerful bacteria that break down grease, grime, and dirt, saving you money on maintenance. Be sure to approve this with your municipal utilities provider.

Your goal should be to have a low percentage of oil, grease, and solid waste in your grease interceptor. This will reduce the number of times you have to pump as well as possible fines and surcharges from your utility department. Many of the cities in which I have worked, mandated that a minimum of 75 percent of water must be present inside grease interceptors. That means the remaining of 25 percent will be composed of oil, grease, solid waste, and other sediments. Be sure to check with your utilities department for regulations specific to your business.

In my last restaurant, by using the services of a professional company using Bio Klean, recycling 100 percent of the used frying oil, and modifying the behavior of the cooks, I was able to reduce the cost associated with sewage pumping by *half*. Before I made any changes, the average cost of pumping was $337 each month (at twelve per year). By adding Bio Klean at a cost of $82 per month we reduced the number of monthly pumpings to three per year. Therefore, the cost went from $337 x 12 = $4044 per year, to $82 x 12 = $984 + $337 + $337 + $337 = $1,995; I saved $2,049!

Light Green **Tips:**

- Install drain screens in sinks and floor drains then dump the debris in the trash can.

- Request a water audit by a technician from your local city utilities department.
- Have your lines, grease traps, and grease interceptor professionally checked and treated with bacteria once a month.

Dark Green Tip:

- If your grease interceptor is more than fifteen years old or not very efficient, have it inspected by your city water utility department and make the recommended or mandatory changes and repairs immediately.

Remember: Cutting down on sewage saves clean water. It takes three gallons of clean water to clean up after releasing one gallon of sewage water!

5.3 Electricity

Investigate and quantify how your electric usage is distributed. In general, businesses use electricity for a great deal of activities: lighting, appliances, equipment, cooling, HVAC, computers and other office devices, and so on. Clearly, electricity is a large and important subject. Additionally, a lot of electrical equipment uses other sources of energy and utilities, which means that you will need to address each one of them specifically, such as electric lighting. Several sections of this guide will address electrical concerns. Again, understanding your usage, your utility bill, and the coincident peak demand for your area is critical to controlling the amount you pay for electricity. Find out from your provider how much you are paying for electricity during coincident peaks hours versus non-coincident peak hours.

Light Green **Tips:**

- Know your coincident peak hours.
- Eliminate phantom electrical loads (this occurs when devices use electricity even though they are turned off or in standby mode).
- Unplug appliances that are not in use.

- Set computers to energy-saver mode.
- Lease an efficient electronic sign for your business.

Dark Green Tip:

- Buy Energy Star–rated appliances.

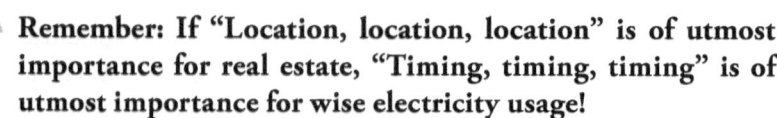

Remember: If "Location, location, location" is of utmost importance for real estate, "Timing, timing, timing" is of utmost importance for wise electricity usage!

5.4 Natural Gas

Natural gas is considered a clean source of energy when the equipment in which it is used is in good working condition.

For example, for heating systems, if you choose a furnace that uses natural gas and connects to a network of ducts, you will have a heat-delivery system that starts with a furnace and delivers heat throughout the inside of your building using that network of ducts. Not only should your furnace be serviced regularly to ensure optimal efficiency, but your thermal envelope—walls, floors, attic, basement, crawl space, windows, doors, ducts, vents—be adequately sealed and insulated! If all aspects of the heating system are working in concert, the amount of natural gas used will be the lowest possible.

This concept is true for other appliances as well. Inspect and maintain hot water heaters *and* their delivery systems, dryers *and* their ventilation systems, ranges *and* their supply lines, etc.

Light Green **Tips:**

- Use your equipment only when necessary.
- Keep your equipment in very clean condition.
- Contract the services of a professional maintenance company.

Dark Green Tip:

- Whenever feasible, invest in a high-efficiency option.

 Remember: Saving gas is just about creating new habits!

5.5 Alternative Sources of Energy

You've probably heard of many, if not all, of these environmentally friendly, relatively nonpolluting means of generating electricity: geothermal, hydroelectric, wind, solar, tidal, and wave power.

When deciding if an energy source is environmentally friendly, you need to consider more than its pollution potential. How much water does the method use? How much water does it take out of the freshwater resources of a nation, a region, etc.? How much land, especially agricultural land, is compromised or used up with this method? How much wildlife habitat is compromised or used up? What is the carbon footprint of the generating plant? What is the footprint of the distribution or transmission method?

It is possible in many areas of the country to purchase electricity generated by wind, solar power, and other alternative sources. Explore what's available in your area.

Light Green **Tips:**

- Research the alternative energy options available in your area.
- Talk to business owners who currently operate with alternative energy sources.

Dark Green Tips:

- If you have enough sunshine in your area, invest in thermal solar panels for heating your hot water.
- Have a complete building audit performed by a professional alternative energy company to see how alternative energy may help your business.

6.   **Lighting**

Lighting is important, but it is also an area where it is easy to go overboard and waste energy. Use natural lighting wherever possible.

6.1 Electric Lighting

Know your lights! For each space in your business, list the location of the lights, type of fixtures, number of fixtures, number of lamps in each fixture, and the specs on the lamps and ballasts (like brand and wattage). Then you can add up the wattage you're using to calculate the net savings you would realize after installing compact fluorescent bulbs and/or LEDs.

Light Green **Tips:**

- Take advantage of natural day lighting.
- Keep light fixtures clean.
- Use task lighting in the office and whenever appropriate.
- Turn out lights in unoccupied rooms.
- Set up a "Lights on and off" policy for openers and closers; post it next to each switch and on employee information boards, employee schedules, and/or office doors, where appropriate and necessary.
- Mark dimmer switches to appropriate settings for day and night, seasonal use, hours of operation, etc. Do not let employees guess when to use lighting and how much; make the decision along with them.
- Set up lighting zones to match the habits of the cleaning crew rather than turning on all the lights at once and keeping all the lights on.
- Turn off lights in walk-in fridge and freezers, dry storage areas, and other infrequently used rooms (electrical room, boiler room, etc.) when not in use.
- Use CFLs or LEDs instead of incandescent lights and remove unnecessary bulbs. In my last business, I used about 2.5 times fewer kilowatts for lighting after those changes!
- Turn on necessary lights only at the appropriate times— for example, half an hour before opening to the public for entrances. Mark the kitchen lights for use only by those

employees. Use and check timers for outside and decorative lights and have them on only when you are open.

Dark Green Tip:

- Install motion sensor light switches wherever appropriate, especially in rooms used frequently by the public (restroom, coat closet, ice machine room, vending machine room, laundry room, bicycle room, etc.).

6.2 Electric Signage

Electric signage is where electricity and marketing come together. You don't want to market yourself as a green business by proclaiming it on a flashing electric billboard!

Following World War II, billboards and other large signs next to major motorways became iconic advertisements of the "American way of life." These signs still bring customers in, but they are expensive to operate and use a tremendous amount of electrical energy. If you have one of these signs, I urge you to put a light green or **dark green** option into practice immediately.

Light Green Tips:

- Program the timing wisely, and know when the sun rises and sets throughout the year.
- Lease an efficient electronic sign for your business that uses less electricity.

Dark Green Tip:

- Buy an efficient electronic sign for your business that uses less electricity.

6.3 Nonelectrical Sources of Lighting

It's very tempting to get rid of electric lighting altogether, but that is not always practical. Sunlight, of course, is a great source of nonelectrical lighting, and it's free. The limitation is that it can only be used during the day, and the length of the day and amount of sunlight vary during the year. And, of course, many businesses are open to the public at night.

When you're looking at nonelectrical lighting sources (sunlight, candle power, etc.), consider your business type and hours of operation, and analyze your most cost-effective options.

Light Green **Tip:**

- Maximize your natural lighting with sunlight as much as possible during the day. If you already have skylights, you may be able to use fewer electric lights than you are currently using.

Dark Green Tips:

- Invest in skylights to let as much natural light as possible into your building.
- Invest in roof-mounted equipment that captures sunlight and brings it inside your building.

7.   Chemicals

Chemicals, both harmful and benign, are present in many of the products businesses use every day. Do what you can to ensure that the chemicals you use are as environmentally friendly as possible, and remember: whatever you wash down the drain eventually ends up in rivers, streams, and oceans.

7.1 Cleaning Products

The claim that many of the chemicals used in domestic and commercial cleaning products can harm people and the environment is still being disputed. However, it is generally held to be true that natural products and cleaners do less harm to the environment and are safer for those who use them and are exposed to them. This has led to an explosion of so-called "green" cleaning products.

But exactly what *green* means for such cleaners and solvents is not always clear. This vague definition has allowed many companies to label products as "environmentally friendly" or "green" when they actually do not meet the generally accepted guidelines for other types of green products.[17] This practice is called *greenwashing*:[18] It involves changing the image of a product to make it appeal to environmentally minded consumers when in fact the product is not produced, used, and/or able to be disposed of in an environmentally friendly manner.

So what cleaning products can you feel safe using? First, try to find products that are nontoxic, biodegradable, and made from renewable resources (not petroleum products). Some restaurants use the cleaning products offered by Ecolab thru the Apex Program. From my twenty-nine years in the hospitality industry, I have found that they are cleaning-effective, cost-effective, safer for the user, and safer for the environment compared to other products.

Remember: Don't just throw your old, toxic cleaning products in the trash. Schedule a hazardous waste pickup so they can be disposed of safely.

Light Green **Tips:**

- Use all cleaning chemicals according to the manufacturer's instructions.
- Do not use more of a cleaning chemical or product than is necessary.
- Do not let dirt and grease pile up before you clean it; then it takes more product to clean!

Dark Green Tip:

- Use environmentally safe and biodegradable commercial cleaning products from reputable companies.

Remember: It is easier to clean something that has been cleaned recently rather than clean something that hasn't been cleaned for a very long time!

7.2 Linen

Some businesses, including most restaurants, outsource the service of cleaning their linen. Others, including most hotels, do it themselves. Cost it out and make the decision based on your volume.

Light Green **Tips:**

- Use a biodegradable cleaning detergent.
- Use an Energy Star-rated washer and dryer.
- Sun-dry linens if at all possible.

Dark Green Tip:

- Use the service of a professional linen company that uses environmentally friendly cleaning products.

7.3 Pest Management

Don't let your customers be distracted by animals and insects that belong outside rather than inside! Your task is to make sure pest control is done as safely, humanely, and with few or no toxic substances.

Integrated pest management is regarded as a more environmentally friendly form of pest control than using traditional pesticides.[19] Its goal is to reduce pesticide use to a minimum by using a variety of less harmful means, with pesticides only as the last resort. *Biological pest control* is another form of control considered by many experts to be environmentally friendly.

The best prevention, of course, is to keep everything as clean as possible!

Light Green **Tips:**

- Keep all areas of your building very clean and organized in order to minimize the attraction of pests.
- Store food in appropriate, sealed dry containers, refrigerators, or freezers.

- Store everything at least six inches above the ground, four inches away from the walls, and eighteen inches away from the ceiling, whenever feasible.

Dark Green Tip:

- Use the services of a professional pest control company that uses environmentally friendly techniques.

7.4 Other Chemical Supplies

For other chemical supplies, use the products and services of a company that develops and markets air deodorizer, water softeners, sanitizers, plumbing maintenance products, and repair products and services for the hospitality, institutional, and industrial markets.

Light Green Tips:

- Use certified products by Green Seal.
- Use harsh chemicals only when you have no other option.

Dark Green Tip:

- Contract with a professional cleaning company that specializes in green and biodegradable cleaning products.

8. Pollution Prevention and Waste Management

Preventing pollution into the air, the rivers and oceans, and the soil is much easier than cleaning it up later. Simply throwing your waste in the trash is now the option of last resort. Your smallest actions can have a huge impact. Recycle, reuse, and do everything possible to leave a light footprint on the earth.

8.1 Waste

You can generally save money and help the environment by reducing the waste you create and increasing your recycling practices. Recycle anything and everything that you can. Again, find out what types of items your local waste management facility collects and/or processes and get on board. Common categories for recycling include paper, cardboard, glass, aluminum, steel, and plastics. Then, properly dispose of all other solid waste.

8.1.1 Solid Waste: Wherever you are located, you probably have a solid waste system in place. Call your local waste hauling company or city office and ask for details. When you use waste services, you can generally save by increasing your recycling and reducing waste in general. As you reduce the sizes of your solid waste containers and the frequency of pickups, you will begin to see substantial savings.

8.1.2 Hood Operations: In businesses with kitchens, the hood takes dangerous fumes and particles from inside the kitchen to the outside of the building. This produces a form of waste that constitutes potential air pollution. Be responsible! Make sure your hood is doing its job efficiently and effectively.

Light Green **Tips:**

- Have your kitchen hood professionally serviced on a quarterly or even monthly basis.
- Once a day, clean the visible parts of the hood and the filters.
- Do not turn on kitchen hoods earlier than necessary, and turn them off as soon as possible at the end of the shift.

Dark Green Tips:

- Have your hood inspected by a professional company, and follow the new recommendations.
- Redesign your hood or change the placement of pollutant emitting equipment to underneath the main force of the hood system if necessary.

8.1.3 Storm Water Pollution: Storm water pollution affects the food we eat. Dangerous contaminants, such as pesticides, motor oil, pet waste, cleaners, and other harmful pollutants, get into storm drains, contaminating our waterways and polluting the environment. Even small traces add up, and it all comes back to you and your family.

Light Green **Tips:**

- Never pour *any form of trash* down a storm drain.
- If waste is potentially toxic, schedule a hazardous waste pickup.
- Sweep your walkways and outdoor public areas near your business rather than hosing waste down the drain.

8.2 Cooking Oil

Throwing used cooking fats and oils down the drain is, thankfully, a thing of the past. Today, there exists a great selection of recycling options from which to choose: from waste hauling companies for solid waste and even cooking oil, to full-service companies that deliver new oil and recycle your old oil, and even to people who would be happy to transform used fryer oil into environmentally friendly biofuel.

Light Green **Tips:**

- Make sure you and your staff use efficient operational kitchen recycling habits.
- Use the services of a specialized company that deals with recycling used oil.
- Have a recycling container specially set up for fryer oil and a program or plan in place for recycling it.
- Find biofuel users or manufacturers in your community who would be happy to take your used cooking oil off your hands.

Dark Green Tip:

- Use the services of a cooking oil company program to deliver and recycle oil regularly.

8.3 Composting

Even when you have to throw out the last scraps of food you can't use, it doesn't have to go to waste. You can compost it! If you have a garden, you can use the compost there to grow more fruits and vegetables and cut your costs even more.

When it comes to composting green waste, you have two options: do it yourself, or hire someone to do it for you. If you make your own compost, you can take it directly from the compost heap to your garden or landscaping. If you employ a specialized company to compost for you, they will provide a container, and you will need to schedule the pickup date. In both cases, you can save money on fertilizers for other areas by using the compost.

Light Green Tip:

- Do the composting yourself in a simple compost heap in your garden. If you are growing an organic garden, be sure you put only organic waste in your compost.

Dark Green Tips:

- Hire a composting company to pick up your waste and compost it.
- Invest in large composting bins and dedicate an area on your property to do the composting.

9. Landscape and Gardening

If your business has any type of vegetation or landscaping associated with it, proper watering and maintenance of that landscaping is important. You can minimize expenses associated with landscaping and gardening by choosing plants native to your local climate and by avoiding wasting water.

Nationally, the EPA states that 50 to 70 percent of household water goes to outdoor watering.[20] According to the Northern Colorado Water Conservancy District, Coloradoans, for instance, water their landscapes extensively to keep them lush and green in the state's arid climate. The result, two-thirds of the drinkable water they use goes to watering outdoors, mostly to water lawns. Even worse, a good portion of this water is wasted through incorrect watering.[21] (Read on for specific tips!) Landscapes composed of non-native plants or from wetter regions consume even more!

No matter where your business is located, if you are concerned about saving water (and I hope you are!), you can convert all or part of your landscaping into a low-maintenance xeriscape—a type of landscape that can cut your water use up to 75 percent while simultaneously reducing the environmental costs of lawn care.

Light Green **Tips:**

- Use commercial water rebates available in your area. (Check with your utilities company.)
- Consult with your local landscape nursery for information on plant selection and placement for optimum outdoor water savings.
- Use Water Sense–labeled products.

Dark Green Tip:

- Obtain a professional water audit.

9.1 Xeriscaping

Xeriscaping, or "dry landscaping," conserves water through creative landscaping techniques originally developed for drought-afflicted areas. With water now considered an expensive and limited resource, landscaping projects in all parts of the country can benefit from this alternative. Xeriscapes do not have a single look, and almost any landscaping style can be achieved.

The financial and environmental benefits of xeriscaping are impressive:

- You can save water—from 50 percent to 75 percent of what you are now using.
- It requires less maintenance and watering.
- Use of native plants eliminates the need for fertilizers and pesticides.
- It improves your property value.
- It is pollution free and reduces the amount of lawn that needs mowing (which most of the time uses gas or electricity).
- It provides wildlife habitat through use of native plants and shrubs.

For an excellent summary of xeriscaping and its principles, visit: http://eartheasy.com/grow_xeriscape.htm

Light Green **Tips:**

- Survey your landscaping to see if you already have native or drought-tolerant plants in place.
- Work with your local nursery to begin transforming your landscaping into a rock garden or to include more drought-tolerant plants.

Dark Green Tip:

- Hire a landscape firm that specializes in xeriscaping to transform your property.

9.2 Turf

Many people are moving away from the large, rolling lawns of the past—and for good reason. Lawns use up a lot of water, and they can be a source of pollution through lawn chemicals. In addition, large lawns mowed with gas mowers burn fuel and create more pollution.

The first step is to ask yourself some questions: Do you really need a lawn? What will it be used for? What kind of maintenance and care are you willing to give it? How much water will you need to use to keep it green? Once you've thought about these things, you may decide you don't really need turf at all.

- But if you do wish to keep some turf on your property, it is possible to do it in a way that is environmentally sound. For one, you can choose grass that is appropriate for you region and uses less water. Many municipalities have information on different types of grasses or you can visit one of many websites sponsored by national companies that have region specific tips. One example is www.yardcare.com.

Another way to reduce water is simply to reduce the size of your lawn, adding decorative beds with plants that require less water. Or consider the use of ornamental grasses or groundcovers—or even synthetic turf—instead of standard turf grass.

Remember: Saving water is saving energy!

Light Green **Tips:**

- Check regularly for broken or missing sprinkler heads. Make sure sprinklers are adjusted properly to water your lawn—not the building, the sidewalk, or the street.
- Water late in the evening or early in the morning.
- Don't water your lawn on windy days, when most of the water blows away or evaporates; sprinkler performance and efficiency decrease rapidly as wind speed increases.
- Rather than following a set watering schedule, check for soil moisture two to three inches below the surface before watering.
- Water only when your lawn shows the need. A change of color and foot prints that remain for a long time indicate a thirsty lawn.
- Water less frequently but thoroughly to promote root growth, which allows the lawn to benefit more from rainfall.
- If just a small area is dry, water that spot by hand.
- If water runs off your lawn easily, split your watering time into shorter periods to allow for better absorption.
- Use a "smart" irrigation controller with a weather monitor for your sprinkler system; the rainfall sensor can detect rain water, and the system won't run when it is raining.
- Convert from traditional spray heads to rotary nozzle heads to reduce evaporation.

Dark Green Tips:

- Increase the number of plant beds you have to reduce turf area.
- Choose shrubs and groundcovers instead of turf for hard-to-water areas, such as steep slopes and isolated strips.
- Use drip irrigation wherever appropriate.
- Use subterranean irrigation for lawn areas (a grid system).

- Convert to a xeriscape landscaping, use rock garden landscaping, or use artificial grass (avoid artificial grasses containing high levels of lead).
- Use professionally installed irrigation controllers, timers, and sensors.
- Use sub-meters for multiple users.
- Use flow meters for users at the irrigation tap.

Remember: A xeriscape or rock garden will also save you maintenance labor costs!

10. Transportation

Transportation is a subject of concern every time we face an energy crisis, but it should actually be of concern to you every day. The cost of energy, mainly fossil fuel, affects the food chain, our employees, and our customers, and therefore it directly affects the way we run our businesses. By their nature, hospitality and retail businesses will always be sensitive to change and crisis in this area.

Protect your business from these changes by planning green from the beginning:

- For employees: Post bus schedules and provide carpooling and vanpooling information. To go greener, encourage biking to work, and provide path maps and bike racks. (If possible, offer bike commuters the option to use a shower before their shift.)
- For customers: Promote and reward their green behavior— make them part of the changes! For example, reward customers who arrive at your business by bicycle or public transportation.
- For your business: Buy locally produced products that do not have to be shipped over long distances.

Light Green **Tips:**

- Save fuel by combining errands into one trip rather than multiple small trips.

- Ride a bicycle or take public transportation to work.
- Walk as much as possible rather than driving short distances.
- Keep your tires properly inflated. This improves gas mileage.

Dark Green Tips:

- Buy or lease a fuel-efficient hybrid or electric vehicle to use for your business (if not also for home!).
- Convert your business vehicle to biofuel and use recycled oil from a restaurant kitchen to power it.

11. Marketing

Doing good is good for business—and that includes your marketing strategy. Now and as in the past, many marketing efforts have been expensive and wasteful, as you likely know from the number of your brochures and flyers that end up in the trash or littering the sidewalk. Thankfully, this is becoming less and less common as sustainable marketing becomes a strong part of the green revolution.

Sustainable marketing takes the life-cycle approach—from designing better and more sustainable products to finding sustainable ways to build sales in your business. It also helps to communicate the ideals of sustainability to others and to inspire them. This can be accomplished through branding, internet marketing, market coalition building, creating new business models, sales building, business development, and by demonstrating, educating, and promoting sustainability.

Sustainability as a Strategy

Sustainable marketing is strategy. Green marketing must happen before and along with the implementation of your green changes. As you make the transition to sustainable marketing, you should adopt these three important strategies:

1. **Build a sustainable strategy and organization.** If you are genuine and authentic, you want to stand out from the crowd. Your corporate identity, business model, and culture must be in sync, and your customers should have a consistent experience. From your Green Team to your Green Policy, such

consistency is what we've been talking about throughout *The Green Guide*.

2. **Do more with fewer marketing resources.** In times when marketing budgets have been cut across the board, marketers need to come up with creative new strategies. Practical performance management tools allowing marketers to track the financial Return on Marketing Investment (ROMI) are crucial. The importance of ROMI will become most evident when and whenever post-crisis related corrective actions have been implemented.

3. **Define, create, and capture more value and margins.** Highlighting product or service value-adds is also crucial. Get your basics right before launching into the latest buzzwords and marketing tricks. Don't be guilty of greenwashing!

The Laws of Marketing

Management is variable, but the laws of marketing—sustainable or otherwise—are not. Before I studied hospitality management, I obtained a degree in marketing. I strongly believe that choosing and using the right marketing strategy and tools will give you a much better chance of success in business—and in greening your business!

Read The 22 Immutable Laws of Marketing by Al Ries and Jack Trout. Violate them at your own risk![22]

Reward Loyalty!

Enticing a new customer to come in is the first challenge. Creating ongoing customer loyalty is the second. One example of sustainable marketing is using an electronic-based, rather than paper based, customer rewards and loyalty program. For several of the businesses that I have worked with, we chose a gift and rewards card system from a company called Finders Keepers. We issued our customers cards made from recycled plastic with magnetic strips on the backs. The cards are non-credit cards capable of running prepaid gifts, rewards, and fundraising applications. The customers receive cash-back incentives to continue to visit us, and if they link their cards to nonprofit organizations, we make donations every time they come in!

When the cards are activated by consumers online or by phone, your business collects valuable marketing data and uses it to communicate with customers by e-mail and mobile text messaging resulting in an increase of your ROMI. And everything is electronic and totally Green!

Why Rewards Work

Rewards work for several reasons:

1. Customers want to be valued, and now you can show them how valuable they are.
2. Customers want to save each time they spend. Now you can increase their spending in a relevant way.
3. You can analyze and develop your marketing initiatives by learning your customers' shopping behavior using an interactive database.

Remember: Traditional marketing is expensive, often ineffective, and wasteful. Green marketing is economical, cost-effective, and sustainable!

Light Green **Tips:**

- Use a green marketing product and service. For instance the Finders Keepers Card, an electronic rewards and gift card system, is one way to acquire and retain customers. (Finders Keepers is a proud sponsor of the Institute of Ecolonomics. See www.FindersKeepersCard.com.)
- Update your website frequently, and publicize your green transformation. Start a blog, use social and professional on-line media, too.
- Use other free or low-cost external marketing to publicize your business: local events, press releases, Chamber of Commerce, and social networking sites, for example.
- Participate in free fairs and conventions, such as Green Summit, Sustainable Living Fairs, Earth Day (April 22), Bike to Work Day (in May), America Recycles Day (November 15), and Energy Awareness Month (October).

Dark Green Tip:

- Use the inexpensive light green marketing solutions unless you have a lot of money to waste!

4. Accounting

As the decision makers inside a business, business owners understand the usual definition of accounting: "The art of analyzing the financial position and operating results of a business house from a study of its sales, purchases, overhead, etc."[23] The interesting part is what happens when we add the word *green* to that.

Green (or sustainable) accounting factors environmental costs into the financial results of a business operation. It is a practical approach that considers life-cycle analysis (the full life of the product from its origin to its sale) along with traditional financial accounting. It considers both the financial factors and the social and environmental factors for any new project with the goal of being both profitable and sustainable.

Just as you began your efforts to take your business green by tracking your costs over the course of a year, continue tracking your costs to learn how much you are saving with your implementation of green practices! Then move on to *sustainable accounting*. Use this approach for new projects as well as ongoing concerns. Traditionally, when you make a decision to invest in a new project that involves a long period of time (say, five to ten years), you may only consider the financial costs of this project. Using sustainable accounting, you must ask:

- Does this project have a sustainable impact?
- Will this project be profitable during its life-cycle?

If you say yes to these two questions, that means this financial project is *ecolonomical*—both sustainable and profitable. Life-cycle analysis considers the full life of the product from its origin: from sourcing, to manufacturing, logistics, marketing, and sales.

When shopping for equipment and supplies and the like, budget-conscious companies are always looking for the cheapest price. However, the cheapest product is rarely the most cost-effective option. Such products are usually made with inferior parts that quickly wear out and cannot be replaced. Cheap design also usually precludes effective recycling of components. Instead, it makes sense to invest in well-designed, more durable items that can be repaired, upgraded, reused, and recycled. Ask your suppliers about their preparedness to take back products at the end of their life for reuse or recycling and also about what in-house practices they have adopted to improve their environmental performance. The more we ask each other these questions, the faster we will move toward making environmentally sustainable business decisions and experience more profit.

The Dish Machine Example

In one of my restaurants, I had a twelve-year-old dish machine that wasted a lot of water and energy, used harsh chemicals, and was very expensive to keep running. Buying a new one using traditional accounting criteria was impossible, because I didn't have the cash and could not get a loan to make the purchase. On the other hand, keeping the old one was very inefficient and very expensive. So I used a more ecolonomical approach.

Old Machine Yearly Costs:

Acquisition	$0
The machine had already been paid for, and its value had depreciated.	
Harsh chemicals	$6,000
Repair and maintenance	$4,000
Labor (66 man-hours weekly)	$30,720
Utilities (water and energy)	$8,000
Estimated at 10% of my utilities bill.	
Total yearly cost	<u>$48,720</u>
Environmental costs: very high!	

New Machine Yearly Costs:

Acquisition, through lease	$2,582
This is the leasing contract.	
Safer chemicals	$9,270

More expensive but also more effective.
Repair and maintenance $0
Ecolab, from whom I leased the machine, is responsible for these expenses.
Labor (47 man-hours weekly) $22,032
The machine is much more efficient and needs less labor to operate.
Utilities (water and energy) $4,600
New utility bills with new savings estimation.
Total yearly cost: $38,484
Environmental costs: much lower!
Yearly savings: $48,720 – $38,484 = $10,236

The conclusion is that leasing a new machine is more green and economical—more ecolonomical!

Now, add even more factors into your life-cycle analysis concept:

Life Cycle Costs include financial costs (leasing, interest, sales tax, property tax), as well as operational costs that include utilities (water, sewage, electric, natural gas,) chemicals, supplies, labor, uniforms, repair and maintenance, waste, recycling, disposal costs, and depreciation. In addition, there are social costs such as working conditions, employee health and safety, human rights and equal opportunity, growth of the local economy, support for social enterprises, support for a sustainable local economy, and fair trade. Finally, bear in mind ecological costs involving resource reduction, waste prevention and reduction, pollution and toxin reduction, and levels of greenhouse gas emissions!

While you can determine the financial bottom line with a thorough cost benefit analysis that reflects the total cost of ownership giving you the real product life-cycle cost, consider adding in social and ecological costs to move toward a "triple bottom line" (TBL) approach.

Sustainability in Action

What Is Triple Bottom Line Accounting?

The phrase "triple bottom line accounting" was coined by John Elkington and further explained in his 1998 book, *Cannibals with Forks: The Triple Bottom Line of 21st Century Business.*[24] Broadly, the concept takes into consideration environmental and social responsibility in addition to financial or economic parameters. It is also referred to as "people, planet, profit," which abstractly illustrates the TBL objective of environmental sustainability.

Globally, the concept of TBL certainly appears to be the direction that business is moving. Whether we, as business people, formally adopt TBL or simply utilize its philosophy to the best of our abilities, at least we will be that much further ahead of the game instead of being just another business ignoring responsibility.

Whatever your decision philosophy when buying a product, make it together with a financial advisor preferably one who uses some sort of sustainable accounting or TBL. Then formulate your business plan, keeping in mind:

- How long will it take to fully realize the benefits?
- Who is going to do it?
- Is it sustainable and not harmful to the environment?

What is most important is to analyze and understand all aspects of your project during its entire life cycle.

Light Green **Tips:**

- Do financial and profit-and-loss overviews. Review last year's history (utilities, waste management, maintenance, supplies, and so on) and set some new goals.
- Progress to making decisions through cost benefit analysis and triple bottom line accounting purposefully adding in sustainable concerns as you go.

Dark Green Tips:

- Research and ask for help getting rebates, loans, grants, and other major financial investments.
- Commit to triple bottom line accounting by writing the concept into your company policy.

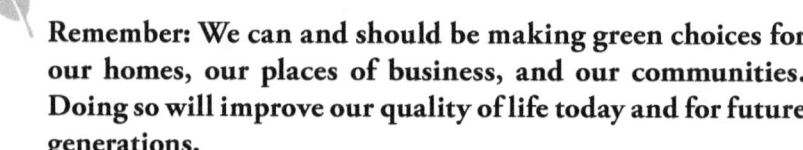

Remember: We can and should be making green choices for our homes, our places of business, and our communities. Doing so will improve our quality of life today and for future generations.

Step 4

Create Your Green Action Plan

Now that you've reviewed your current ecolonomic status, it's time to create an action plan—light green and **dark green** changes that will make your business green and sustainable. Ready? Let's get started.

List Your Options

Meet with your Green Team and identify opportunities, room for improvement, challenges, a wish list, and your preferences for each area. For example:

- You've probably found a number of opportunities to turn off lights, use natural light in place of electricity, water your landscape less, recycle waste, and more.
- You may have found room for improvement in your recycling program.
- You may have a wish list that includes replacing your dish machine or buying a truck that can run on biofuel recycled from oil in your fryer.
- You may have discovered a preference for xeriscaping over your current water-consuming landscape.

Use the list at the beginning of Step 3 to help you remember all the categories.

Identify Your "Smart" Goals

You probably have quite a list for greening things up, but you can't do everything all at once. So identify the real opportunities—the ones that are worth your time, money, and effort to focus on first. Set up specific "smart" goals in each area. Keep your goals simple, specific, measurable, and attainable. For example:

Energy:
- Reduce heating bills.
- Reduce electric bills.
- Explore alternative energy sources.

Landscape:
- Use less water monthly.
- Explore drought-tolerant landscaping options.
- Replace lawns with rock gardens.

If necessary, hire professionals to do technical and financial assessments on potential projects that are more complex and expensive.

Make Your Light Green and Dark Green Lists

Finally, organize your targets into priority groups:

- **Light Green:** Changes you can begin doing immediately for little or no cost.
- **Dark Green:** More complex or costly changes that take time and money to implement.

For example, your light green list might have these items:

- Replace incandescent light bulbs with energy-saving bulbs.
- Purchase local products rather than products shipped long distances.
- Turn off lights when not in use.

Your **dark green** list might have these items:

- Purchase Energy Star–rated equipment for the laundry room.
- Hire a landscaper to xeriscape, and invest in a water-saving irrigation system for the rest of the landscaping.

Finalize Your Action Plan

This is the final step, so make sure you have all your facts:

- Review your assessment results and data.
- Identify the changes that need to be made.
- Prioritize the light green and **dark green** lists.
- Finally, move on to Step 5: implementing your changes for a greener future!

If you have a mentor, bring him or her back into this final discussion.

Remember: It is easier to focus on the 10 percent of things that will provide 90 percent of the green impact than to focus on the 90 percent of things that will provide that last 10 percent of your impact!

Step 5

Implement Your Green Action Plan

Now you can begin making changes! To keep everyone motivated—including yourself—start with the top five to ten targets that will impact your business positively and quickly. Both light green and **dark green** changes will have some sustainable impact.

What is most important is to begin with something *today*. Tomorrow you can make more choices about what areas you want to improve. There is always room for improvement—there are no limitations.

Make it easy on yourself; don't try to do everything at once. Prioritize the ten areas that have the greatest impact on your bills or where your assessments show you have the most room for improvement. Then choose the top few of these ten that you want to work on in the first month, and implement your plan. Do it with the full and genuine intent to make successful improvements. Document the facts and numbers and then analyze the results.

In my last business, and also at home, I implemented one change per month—quantifying it, documenting it, and then analyzing it. In some cases, I was very surprised to find out that what I thought would be very easy to improve was really quite difficult. At the same time, some changes that initially seemed insignificant (like the 89 cent black marker technique) made a very big difference in the long term. Don't assume! Get real data on every change you implement.

Step 6

Document Your Success

After you have implemented your highest priority changes and lived with them for a while, you may feel that your green changes are having a real effect ... but you won't know for certain without documenting your success.

You reviewed your consumption and spending before you began making light green and **dark green** improvements, so you have a great baseline from which to measure. Keep collecting this data! Soon, the figures should tell you that:

- Your consumption is decreasing.
- Your waste is decreasing.
- Your expenses are decreasing (and budgeted properly!)
- Your costs are lowering.
- Your business is starting to have a neutral or positive effect on the environment rather than a damaging effect.
- Your customers are noticing and approving of your stance on sustainability.

Don't stop documenting your success! You probably have many more changes to implement, so keep monitoring your progress:

- Are your changes being implemented properly?
- Are changes being implemented in an organized way?
- Are you improving your quality of operations?
- Are you paying attention to details?
- Are you tracking your costs and savings?

By fully answering these questions, you can assess the effectiveness of your teams' efforts. You can also target additional or new areas of concern and further improvement.

And don't forget your Green Team; their efforts help make your successes possible. Be sure to:

- Reward your Green Team, managers, and employees for their light green behavior changes.
- Recognize the efforts of your consultants and let them know you appreciate them.

Now comes the fun part: Share your results! Let others know how effective your efforts have been and continue to be. And consider keeping the green cycle moving forward by mentoring another business through this process.

 Remember: You can't manage what you can't measure!

Step 7

Be a Mentor

You've done it. Congratulations!

Now it's time to pass along to others what you have learned. Becoming a green business is a sustainable process; you are part of a cycle. When you become a mentor, you pass along the knowledge you have gained and ensure that the green business cycle continues.

You have what it takes to be a mentor:

- Mentors are people who care about seeing the green cycle continue.
- Mentors act as positive examples of what can be done.
- Mentors provide business owners and entrepreneurs with support, counsel, friendship, reinforcement, and practical advice.

Plus, mentors learn more by teaching others! Learning never stops with increasing experience.

Promoting environmentally friendly practices in your community through information, education, and mentoring, as well as by the practical example of your own successful green and sustainable business, will empower others to make green choices and therefore enhance your own life and those of your family and fellow community members.

Remember: Green is the only color that our blue planet can accept in order to ensure what is most important to us all: life itself!

Growing Your Green Business

Long-Term Benefits of Sustainability

As soon as you make your first light green change, you should start realizing the benefits of greening your business. Yet the long-term benefits of sustainability are even more dramatic.

Financial:
- Cutting back on energy use, waste, and other costs will save you money in the short term and the long term.
- Your enhanced image in the business community will bring in more customers, increasing your sales.

Efficiency of your operation:
- Savings on utilities will reduce your waste and provide more money for making greater changes in the future.
- Your Green Team will have renewed loyalty to your organization.

Environmental:
- You'll reduce your carbon footprint, your waste, and the overall harm you do to the environment.
- You will be actively helping the environment to heal past damage.

Keep Going!

For a sustainable and profitable economy in hospitality, retail, and home businesses, the long-term benefits must be environmentally friendly and ongoing. Very responsible commercial **dark green** behavior includes:

- Being supplied with 100 percent renewable energy.
- Creating a zero-solid-waste environment.
- Minimizing greenhouse gas emissions or offsetting carbon use with proper carbon-free investments.
- Selling only products that sustain the environment rather than damage it.

In addition, you must read your expenses budget with fresh eyes:

- Use your repair and maintenance budget to finance your light green expenses.
- Use the savings generated by reducing utilities to reinvest in more green changes.
- Spend wisely on preventive maintenance in order to avoid expensive repairs.
- Remove your expensive and inefficient advertising budget, and switch to an efficient and cost-effective loyalty and rewards marketing program that drives active consumer participation.

These days, funding sources are friendly to businesses interested in making green and sustainable improvements. Look into funding energy efficiency upgrades through:

- Public and private funding
- Subsidies
- Bank loans (using typical loan products)
- Specialized energy efficiency loans
- Grants(government, municipal, or Downtown Development Association)
- Private or philanthropic grants or gifts
- Federal, state, and local government tax incentives
- Rebates from manufactures, utilities, and government entities

To realize long-term benefits, you must embrace a true **Dark Green** approach. This, of course, takes financial resources. Grants and special loans may make your changes more affordable. Every state has programs available to help, some more than others. Spend a few moments to research programs in your area, and you may be pleasantly surprised. For example, at the time of the writing of this book, I found over forty federal, state, and local programs for funding green investments in my area alone. Websites such as www.dsireusa.org (the Database of State Incentives for Renewables and Efficiency), sponsored by the US Department of Energy, are great resources. And remember to check with your local utilities providers!

 Remember: Waste is profitability in the wrong direction!

Conclusion: Your Green Future

Now that you have used this guide, you understand that "being green" is not just a catchphrase or a passing fad. Not only can being green generate more profit, it can improve your operations!

If you've already moved from a light green to a **dark green** approach, you have learned how to conserve energy and possibly even to neutralize energy and natural resource usage. Let us all become such experts that we can tackle the next step: repairing the damage already done to our environment and creating a healthy world for our grandchildren.

Green Resources

The Institute of Ecolonomics

The Institute of Ecolonomics (IOE) is a 501(c)(3) organization founded by the late actor and environmental activist, Dennis Weaver. Mr. Weaver wanted to leave a legacy based on more than just his fifty-year career in film and television. With a passion for preserving our planet, Mr. Weaver set out to demonstrate that a symbiotic relationship existed between a healthy ecology and a strong economy. He believed this relationship was the only formula for a sustainable future and that these two goals were two sides of the same coin.

Mr. Weaver spoke to CEOs in both camps, urging them to work together toward proving that tremendous profit was available for the taking by doing the right thing: preserving our natural resources. His conclusion was that until this message was embraced, we would continue to destroy the most vital components of our world that sustain life: the air, water, and soil.

Since it was established in 1993, the Institute of Ecolonomics has solely focused on exploiting necessary green technologies by launching them into the marketplace. IOE facilitates this action by providing third-party applied research, market research, business plans, and assembly of administrative leadership as well as by raising capital. Ultimately, IOE's reputation is seen as advantageous to the success of new products or technologies entering the market to satisfy consumer demand.

Mr. Scott Fardulis is currently the chairman and CEO of the Institute of Ecolonomics. Mr. Fardulis was an IOE board member for many years and has recently stepped up to lead the organization and direct its activities. His effectiveness in leadership has been recognized in prominent affiliations with Our Children International, Monarch Youth Homes, and the Institute of Ecolonomics. With a gift for assembling cohesive teams and empowering and equipping all ranks of leaders, Mr. Fardulis has been instrumental in building and growing sustainable organizations.

Mr. Bruno Gerard Krioussis, current IOE Vice President of Operations, recently joined the Institute of Ecolonomics and brings a unique skill set to the team. He was born in Iran, was raised in Africa, studied in France, has Greek heritage, has lived in thirty-five countries, and speaks three languages fluently and has studied four others. After twenty-nine years in the hospitality and food service industries, he is recognized as a culinary instructor as well as a food and beverage consultant on an international level, and has been the host of a television cooking show. Mr. Krioussis is considered an acclaimed consultant for merchants, and he specializes in alternative energy implementation in businesses as well as homes. Today he has been a trailblazer in Northern Colorado with the Fort ZED Initiative and the Climate Wise Program.

Online Resources

The following websites have served as inspiration and resources for the content of this guide:

Green Guide Partners

Institute of Ecolonomics (www.ecolonomics.org)

Since it was established in 1993, the Institute of Ecolonomics has solely focused on developing necessary green technologies and launching them into the marketplace.

Climate Wise (www.fcgov.com/climatewise)

"The goal of Climate Wise is to reduce greenhouse gas emissions by promoting waste reduction, energy savings, alternative transportation, water conservation, and pollution prevention in Fort Collins, Colorado."

Fort ZED (www.fortzed.com)

"Fort ZED is growing to be the world's largest active zero energy district. Located in downtown Fort Collins, Colorado, Fort ZED is a collaborative effort, sharing best practices at the state, regional, national, and global levels. Fort ZED is a set of active projects and initiatives, created by public–private partnerships, that uses Smart Grid and renewable energy technologies to achieve local power generation and energy demand management."

Restaurant, Food, and Food Service

Colorado Restaurant Association
(www.coloradorestaurant.com)

"The Colorado Restaurant Association's mission is to represent, educate and promote Colorado's foodservice industry, fostering high standards of business practice and integrity. The CRA is dedicated to providing leadership, advocacy, information and services to enhance the success of our members and the Colorado foodservice industry."

Eat Local (www.eatlocal.net)

When you buy direct from local farmers, your dollars stay within your community, and strengthen the local economy. "More than 90¢ of every dollar you spend goes to the farmer, thus preserving farming as a livelihood and farmland. This is important because as mergers in the food industry have increased, the portion of your food dollar paid to farmers has decreased. Vegetable farmers earn only 21¢ of your dollar; the other 79¢ goes to pay for marketing, distribution, and other costs."

Ecolab (www.ecolab.com)

Ecolab develops and sells cleaning, sanitizing, pest control, maintenance, and repair products and services for the hospitality, institutional, and industrial markets.

"Ecolab has always been counted on for high-performance, one-pass warewashing. Now, with the Apex warewashing System, Ecolab takes it to the next level, delivering a state-of-the-art way to streamline your warewashing procedures, help reduce total dishroom costs, and lower your environmental impact."

Ecolab can also help you meet your goal of providing a pest-free guest experience while reducing your environmental impact. "As the innovation leader, we're continuously improving our products and services to be more sustainable while maintaining Ecolab's high efficacy standards."

Finders Keepers Card (www.finderskeeperscard.com)

The Finders Keepers Card is a non-credit card in the gift and loyalty industry capable of running prepaid gift, rewards, and fundraising applications on a single card, thereby rewarding customers and encouraging them to return to the issuing business.

Going Greener (www.greenrestaurants.org)

Contains opportunities and tips for improving your restaurant's environmental practices.

Green Restaurant Association (www.dinegreen.com)

"The Green Restaurant Association is a national nonprofit organization that provides a convenient and cost-effective way for restaurants, manufacturers, distributors, and consumers to become more environmentally responsible."

Local Harvest (www.localharvest.org)

Use this website to locate farms, Community Supported Agriculture (CSA,) and attend events in your state involving locally grown organic goods.

Northern Colorado Food Incubator
(www.NoCoFoodIncubator.com)

"The Northern Colorado Food Incubator (NCFI) is dedicated to a Living Economy: locally sustainable and globally fair. Working collaboratively, we support independent community- and land-based businesses and advocate for a whole, resilient community and bio-region. We provide support, guidance and assistance to food-related businesses and entrepreneurs in Northern Colorado."

EnergyStar (www.energystar.com)

Find links on what it means to be EnergyStar, energy efficient products, home improvements, new homes and more.

CEE (www.cee1.org)

"CEE is a consortium of efficiency program administrators from across the U.S. and Canada who work together on common approaches to advancing efficiency. Through joining forces, the individual efficiency programs of CEE are able to partner not only with each other, but with other industries, trade associations, and government agencies. By working together at CEE, administrators leverage the effect of their funding dollars, exchange information on effective practices and, by doing so, achieve greater energy efficiency for the public good."

Food Service Technology Center (www.fishnick.com)

Promotes energy efficiency in food service.

Green Product Labeling

Energy Star (www.energystar.gov)

Energy-saving home and business equipment products are identified with the Energy Star label. Energy Star is a joint program of the US Environmental Protection Agency and the US Department of Energy. Energy Star labeling indicates products that save money and protect the environment through being energy efficient.

Green Seal (www.greenseal.org)

"We develop life cycle-based sustainability standards for products, services and companies and offer third-party certification for those that meet the criteria in the standard. Green Seal has been actively identifying and promoting sustainability in the marketplace, and helping organizations be greener in a real and effective way since 1989."

Lighting

Energy Efficient Systems (www.eesilighting.com)

"Our energy efficient lighting retrofit programs will provide you with better, brighter lighting that is healthier for your eyes, lasts longer, and will save you 40-60% on your monthly lighting expense."

Efficient Windows Collaborative (www.efficientwindows.org)

"Efficient Windows Collaborative (EWC) members have made a commitment to manufacture and promote energy-efficient windows. This site provides unbiased information on the benefits of energy-efficient windows, descriptions of how they work, and recommendations for their selection and use."

International Dark-Sky Association (IDA) (www.darksky.org)

"The mission of the International Dark-Sky Association (IDA) is to preserve and protect the nighttime environment and our heritage of dark skies through environmentally responsible outdoor lighting."

Water Conservation

Fort Collins-Loveland Water District and South Fort Collins Sanitation District (www.fclwd.com)

Northern Colorado Water Conservancy District (www.ncwcd.org)

"...to provide practical information to homeowners, industry and landscape professionals on water conservation and related subjects."

Water Resources Information from the City of Denver, Colorado (www.denverwater.org)

WaterSense Program (www.epa.gov/watersense)

"WaterSense, a partnership program sponsored by the US Environmental Protection Agency, makes it easy for Americans to save water and protect the environment. Look for the WaterSense label to choose quality, water-efficient products. Many products are available, and don't require a change in your lifestyle."

Landscaping

Irrigation Association (www.irrigation.org)

"The Irrigation Association is the leading membership organization for irrigation companies and professionals. Together with our members, we are committed to promoting efficient irrigation and to long-term sustainability of water resources for future generations."

Xeriscape Information from the City of Fort Collins (www.fcgov.com/xeriscape)

Xeriscaping and other sustainable solutions (eartheasy.com)

Building

Building Green (www.buildinggreen.com)

Information about sustainable building practices and products.

Colorado Home Energy Solutions (www.thisefficienthouse.com)

Solutions about how to use energy in your home.

Is your Home Energy Efficient? (www.livingzero.org)

Living Zero homes tour and other energy solutions for your home.

US Green Building Council (www.usgbc.org)

The website of the US Green Building Council (LEED Rating System).

Smart Energy Living Alliance (www.smartenergyliving.org)

Information about renewable energy and energy efficiency in the building industry.

Sustainable Business Practices

Bay Area, California, Green Business Program
(www.greenbiz.ca.gov)

Be Local (www.BeLocalNC.org)

Be Local is "dedicated to a Living Economy: locally-sustainable and globally-fair. We support independent community- and land-based businesses and advocate for a whole, resilient community and bioregion." Be Local also partners with BALLE (see below).

Business Alliance for Local Living Economies (BALLE)
(www.livingeconomies.org)

"North America's fastest growing network of socially responsible businesses, comprised of over 80 community networks with over 21,000 independent business members across the U.S. and Canada."

Center for a Sustainable Economy (CSE)
(www.myfootprint.org)

"CSE works to speed the transition to a sustainable society through rigorous analysis of policy, programs, and projects, by developing creative solutions for government agencies, businesses, nonprofits, and educators, and by providing expert support for legislative, administrative, and legal campaigns."

Environmental Leadership Program
(www.cdphe.state.co.us)

"The Environmental Leadership Program is a statewide environmental recognition and reward program administered by the Colorado Department of Public Health and Environment's Sustainability Program. The Environmental Leadership Program offers benefits and incentives to members that voluntarily go beyond compliance with state and federal regulations and are committed to continual environmental improvement."

Fort Collins Area Chamber of Commerce
(www.fcchamber.org)

Green Business Partnership (GBPP)
(www.scgov.net/greenbusiness)

The Green Business Partnership (GBP) in association with Sarasota County, Florida.

Pay It Green (www.payitgreen.org)

"Paying bills online, getting your statements electronically, or setting up direct deposit benefits the environment we all share by reducing the production, transportation, and disposal of paper."

Redirect Guide (www.redirectguide.com)

The "Healthy and Sustainable Business Directory and Lifestyle Guide" for Portland/Vancouver, Salt Lake City/Park City, and Denver/Boulder/Fort Collins areas.

Responsible Purchasing Network
(www.responsiblepurchasing.org)

"RPN is an international network of buyers dedicated to socially responsible and environmentally sustainable purchasing Network of Buyers."

StartupNation (www.startupnation.com)

"StartupNation is a free service founded *by* entrepreneurs *for* entrepreneurs. We created this site to be your one-stop shop for entrepreneurial success, and we're thrilled that StartupNation has grown to be the leading online content and community resource for entrepreneurs."

Sustainable Business Leader Program (SBLP)
(www.sustainablebusinessleader.org)

Organization servicing the City of Boston, Massachusetts.

Water Footprint Network (www.waterfootprint.org)

Defines and details a water footprint and includes a water footprint calculator.

Sustainability

Alliance for Sustainable Colorado
(www.sustainablecolorado.org)

"The mission of Alliance for Sustainable Colorado is to catalyze the shift to a truly sustainable world by fostering collaboration among nonprofits, businesses, governments, and academia. We are working to advance economic, environmental, and social sustainability in Colorado by building cross-sector alliances and networks."

Be Green Minded (www.begreenminded.com)

"We, BeGreenMinded.com, say it's okay to be wherever you are now in your 'greenness,' and you can still make a difference! We all have to start someplace! We all have room for improvement! You do not have to go from being a polluter to carbon neutral all at once! AND—we do know that each and every person, of whichever race, creed, religion and political affiliation, WANTS to make a difference in this world. We are here to support that."

Center for ReSource Conservation (CRC)
(www.conservationcenter.org)

Boulder, Colorado's, Center for ReSource Conservation (CRC) "implements programs for the community through three divisions: waste, energy, and water. The CRC's mission is to empower our community to conserve natural resources."

City of Madison Green Capitol City Plan
(www.cityofmadison.com/sustainability)

City of Springfield, Illinois, Green Program
(www.springfield.il.us/green)

City of Tucson, Arizona, Office of Conservation and Sustainable Development (www.tucsonaz.gov/ocsd)

Cool California (www.coolcalifornia.org)

Sacramento, California's sustainability implementation plan.

Environment Colorado (www.environmentcolorado.org)

"Environment Colorado is a statewide, citizen-based environmental advocacy organization. Our professional staff combines independent research, practical ideas and tough-minded advocacy to overcome the opposition of powerful special interests and win real results for Colorado's environment. Environment Colorado draws on 30 years of success in tackling our state's top environmental problems."

Greenprint Denver (www.greenprintdenver.org)

"Greenprint Denver, Colorado, is an initiative of the Denver Mayor's Office to promote the importance of sustainable development and ecologically-friendly practices throughout the city."

Larimer County, Colorado, Environment and Natural Resources
(http://www.larimer.org/services/category.cfm?sv_id=12)

Masdar City (www.masdarcity.ae)

An urban development in Abu Dhabi, United Arab Emirates aiming to become one of the most sustainable cities powered by renewable energy.

Partners for a Clean Environment (PACE)
(www.bouldercolorado.gov)

A partnership of local governments and businesses in Boulder, Colorado.

Santa Monica, California, Office of Sustainability and the Environment (www.smgov.net/ose)

Smarter Cities (www.smartercities.nrdc.org/smarter-cities)

A project of the Natural Resources Defense Council (NRDC), a nonprofit 501(c)(3), Smarter Cities "is a multimedia web initiative whose aim is to be a news-you-can-use web portal for and about cities striving to make themselves "smarter" – more efficient, sustainable, equitable and livable."

Portland, Oregon, Bureau of Environmental Services
(http://www.portlandonline.com/bes/index.cfm?c=29323)

Rocky Mountain Sustainable Living Association
(www.SustainableLivingAssociation.org)

Salt Lake City Environmental Program
(www.slcgreen.com)

Alternative, Clean, and Renewable Energy

American Solar Energy Society (www.ases.org)

An association of solar professionals and advocates working "to increase the use of solar energy, energy efficiency and other sustainable technologies in the U.S."

Colorado Renewable Energy Society (CRES)
(www.cres-energy.org)

"The mission of CRES is to inspire an era of clean energy innovation, speeding the transition to sustainable energy economy in Colorado by advancing education, policy, and economic development."

Consortium for Energy Efficiency (CEE)
(www.cee1.org)

"CEE is a consortium of efficiency program administrators from across the U.S. and Canada who work together on common approaches to advancing efficiency. Through joining forces, the individual efficiency programs of CEE are able to partner not only with each other, but with other industries, trade associations, and government agencies. By working together at CEE, administrators leverage the effect of their funding dollars, exchange information on effective practices and, by doing so, achieve greater energy efficiency for the public good."

Database of State Incentives for Renewables and Efficiency (DSIRE) (www.dsireusa.org)

"DSIRE is a comprehensive source of information on state, local, utility and federal incentives and policies that promote renewable energy and energy efficiency. Established in 1995 and funded by the U.S. Department of Energy, DSIRE is an ongoing project of the N.C. Solar Center and the Interstate Renewable Energy Council."

Fort Collins Department of Utilities (www.fcgov.com/utilities)

Although aimed at the City of Fort Collins, Colorado, this site contains much information about conserving water and energy.

Governor's Energy Office (GEO), Colorado (www.colorado.gov/energy)

"The GEO's mission is to lead Colorado to a New Energy Economy by advancing energy efficiency and renewable, clean energy resources. The New Energy Economy embraces energy conservation as an important component in our energy future, yet requires a broader mission to meet the goals of expanding renewable and clean energy resources and opportunities for the state's economy, environment and energy independence."

Green Power Company (www.greenpowercompany.net)

"Green Power Company (GPC) is Colorado's premier provider of low-cost, clean, renewable, electric power to tax-exempt organizations. We bring a true full-service solutions approach to large-scale solar systems including design, engineering, installation, monitoring, maintenance, financing, and assumption of liability so your organization doesn't have to."

Green Power Oregon (greenpoweroregon.com)

The renewable energy and sustainability home page for the City of Portland, Oregon.

Ice Energy (www.ice-energy.com)

"Ice Energy delivers distributed energy storage and smart grid solutions for optimizing energy system efficiency."

Northern Colorado Clean Energy Cluster
(www.nccleanenergy.com)

Northern Colorado Renewable Energy Society
(www.ncres.org)

Project C—Colorado Carbon Fund
(www.coloradocarbonfund.org)

"The Governor's Energy Office created the Project C campaign to help individuals, business owners and event planners measure, reduce, and offset their carbon emissions. In partnership with local governments and organizations around the state, Project C is helping Coloradans do their part to help with climate change. By donating to the Colorado Carbon Fund, you can reduce emissions by helping us support new clean energy projects here in our state."

Radiantec
(www.radiantec.com)

Radiantec has been a leader in radiant heating since 1979.

Sacramento (California) Municipal Utility District (SMUD)
(www.smud.org)

SMUD is nationally recognized as a leader in renewable resources and electric transportation.

Smart Energy Living Alliance (www.SmartEnergyLiving.org)

The Smart Energy Living Alliance helps individuals and businesses make smart energy decisions and ensures qualified professionals are available to support their needs.

Solar Energy International (SEI) (www.solarenergy.org)

"SEI was founded in 1991 as a nonprofit educational organization to help others to use renewable energy resources and sustainable building technologies through education and technical assistance."

Solar Professional Services (www.solarproservices.com)

"Fort Collins's Solar Professional Services provides independent, credible expertise in a comprehensive solar site assessment: pre-installation review, energy efficiency and conservation, financial analysis, purchasing consultation, and third party bid evaluation."

Recycling

A1 Organics (www.a1organics.com)

"A1 Organics has been in the organic recycling and commercial composting business for three decades. Composting and organic recycling is our only business. We do not operate farms, dairies, or even landfills, where organic materials are frequently viewed as a 'waste product,' something of little or no value that needs to be disposed of. No, our business is organic recycling and composting, ultimately producing a high-quality product that is beneficial to the environment."

Colorado Association for Recycling (www.cafr.org)

Search for information and recycling center locations across the State of Colorado.

Ecocyle (www.ecocycle.org)

"We believe in individual and community action to transform society's throw-away ethic into environmentally-friendly stewardship. Our mission is to provide publicly-accountable recycling, conservation and education services, and to identify, explore and demonstrate the emerging frontiers of sustainable resource management."

Facility Cycle (www.facilitycycle.com)

"It's a free, online community resource for business owners, facilities managers, non-profits, commercial real estate professionals, and others who want to help keep their used stuff out of landfills." Buy, sell, trade, donate and recycle items from your facility through this site.

Recycled Products.com (www.recycledproducts.com)

A catalogue of products made of recycled materials as well as education materials on ways to recycle common and difficult items.

Recycled Products Cooperative (www.recycledproducts.org)

This co-op offers a free membership to purchase recycled and environmentally friendly office products.

Alternative Transportation

Smart Trips (www.smarttrips.org)

Use their Commute Cost Calculator. The site also "offers improved rideshare solutions designed for developing a successful alternative transportation program."

National Center for Transit Research at USF (www.bestworkplaces.org)

This site lists the qualifying Best Workplaces for Commuters. "Best Workplaces for Commuters members are nationally recognized leaders offering outstanding commuter benefits to their employees."

Green Ride Company (www.greenrideco.com)

Airport shuttle and charters for Denver International Airport (DIA).

Environment

Colorado Division of Wildlife (www.wildlife.state.co.us)

Earthjustice (www.earthjustice.org)

"Earthjustice is a non-profit public interest law firm dedicated to protecting the magnificent places, natural resources, and wildlife of this earth, and to defending the right of all people to a healthy environment. Earthjustice works through the courts on behalf of citizen groups, scientists, and other parties to ensure government agencies and private interests follow the law."

Climate Analysis (www.earthtrends.wri.org)

Environmental information from the World Resources Institute and the Climate Analysis Indicators Tool (CAIT).

One Planet Vision (www.oneplanetvision.org)

"One Planet Vision is a website from BioRegional that provides tools and inspiration to help companies, organisations and individuals use the One Planet Living framework to live and work within a fair share of the earth's resources."

The Nature Conservancy (www.nature.org)

"The Nature Conservancy has been using science and partnerships to protect earth's most important natural places, for you and future generations."

Wild Lands Restoration Volunteers (www.wlrv.org)

"Wildlands Restoration Volunteers is a non-profit organization that provides an opportunity for people to come together, learn about their natural environment, and take direct action to restore and care for the land."

United States Government Agencies

AIRNow (www.airnow.gov)

Consumer Energy Tax Incentives
(www.energy.gov/print/taxbreaks)

Federal Government Grants (www.grants.gov)

Green Leaf Certification www.epa.gov/smartway

re-TRAC Program (www.epa.gov/wastewise)**Tax Incentives Assistance Project** (www.energytaxincentives.org)

US DOE Energy Efficiency and Renewable Energy (www.eere.energy.gov)

US Environmental Protection Agency (www.epa.gov)

Works Cited

"accounting." *Collins English Dictionary | Complete & Unabridged 10th Edition*. HarpersCollins Publishers. Web. 14 Feb. 2011. <Dictionary.comhttp://dictionary.reference.com/browse/accounting>.

"Be Hydro-Logical | Drinking Water | US EPA." *Index | Water | US EPA*. United States Environmental Protection Agency, 21 Apr. 2010. Web. 11 Feb. 2011. <http://water.epa.gov/learn/kids/drinkingwater/behyrdological.cfm>.

"Complying with the Environmental Marketing Guides." *BCP Business Center*. Federal Trade Commission, May 2000. Web. 11 Feb. 2011. <http://business.ftc.gov/documents/bus42-complying-environmental-marketing-guides>.

"Electricity FAQs - Energy Information Administration." *Independent Statistics and Analysis: U.S. Energy Information Administration*. U.S. Deptment of Energy, 29 Mar. 2010. Web. 11 Feb. 2011. <http://tonto.eia.doe.gov/ask/electricity_faqs.asp#electricity_use_home>.

"FAQs | The Sins of Greenwashing: Home and Family Edition." *The Sins of Greenwashing: Home and Family Edition*. TerraChoice Group Inc, 2011. Web. 11 Feb. 2011. <http://sinsofgreenwashing.org/findings/faqs/>.

"Fish Consumption Advisories for the State of Colorado." *Colorado Department of Public Health and Environment*. Web. 11 Feb. 2011. <http://www.cdphe.state.co.us/wq/FishCon/faqs.html>.

FortZED. Web. 11 Feb. 2011. <http://fortzed.com/>.

Gordon, Wendy. "American Cities Get Smart about Energy | Smarter Cities." *Main | Smarter Cities.* Natural Resources Defense Council, 19 July 2010. Web. 08 Feb. 2011. <http://smartercities.nrdc.org/articles/american-cities-get-smart-about-energy>.

"Integrated Pest Management (IPM) Principles | Fact Sheets | About Pesticides | Pesticides | US EPA." *Pesticides: Topical & Chemical Fact Sheets.* US Environmental Protection Agency, 8 Dec. 2010. Web. 11 Feb. 2011. <http://www.epa.gov/opp00001/factsheets/ipm.htm>.

Pirog, Rick, Timothy Van Pelt, Kamyar Enshayan, and Ellen Cook. "Leopold Center - Food, Fuel, and Freeways." Thesis. Leopold Center for Sustainable Agriculture, 2001. *Leopold Center for Sustainable Agriculture.* June 2001. Web. 11 Feb. 2011. <http://www.leopold.iastate.edu/pubs/staff/ppp/>.

"Population Estimates." *Census Bureau Home Page.* Population Division. Web. 11 Feb. 2011. <http://www.census.gov/popest/archives/>.

"Progress and Results: City of Fort Collins." *City of Fort Collins, Colorado Official Website.* Web. 06 Feb. 2011. <http://www.fcgov.com/climatewise/progress.php>.

Ries, Al, and Jack Trout. *The 22 Immutable Laws of Marketing: Violate Them at Your Own Risk.* New York, NY: HarperBusiness, 1993. Print.

"Summary of RCRA | Laws & Regulations| US EPA." *US Environmental Protection Agency.* 13 Jan. 2011. Web. 11 Feb. 2011. <http://www.epa.gov/lawsregs/laws/rcra.html>.

"The Triple Bottom Line | Strategies & Tools." *Business and Sustainable Development: A Global Guide.* International Institute for Sustainable Development (IISD), 17 Jan. 2000. Web. 16 Feb. 2011. <http://www.iisd.org/business/tools/principles_triple.asp>.

United States. General Accounting Office. *Freshwater Supply States' Views of How Federal Agencies Could Help Them Meet the Challenges of Expected Shortages : Report to Congressional Requesters.* [Washington, D.C.]: U.S. General Accounting Office, 2003. Print.

"US Indoor Water Use | WaterSense | US EPA." *US Environmental Protection Agency.* Office of Waste Water Management. Web. 11 Feb. 2011. <http://www.epa.gov/WaterSense/pubs/indoor.html>.

"Utilities: City of Fort Collins." *City of Fort Collins, Colorado Official Website.* 2011. Web. 14 Feb. 2011. <http://www.fcgov.com/utilities/business/rates/electric/coincident-peak>.

"Water Conservation." *NCWCD Home Page.* The Northern Colorado Water Conservancy District. Web. 12 Feb. 2011. <http://www.ncwcd.org/ncwcd_about/water.asp>.

"Water To Waste Resource Information Section Two: Water Energy Efficiency Information and EPA WaterSense Program." *WasteWater Education.* Web. 11 Feb. 2011. <http://www.wastewatereducation.org/w2w08/w2w08a.html>.

Weaver, Dennis. "Ecolonomics ... Think Anew, Act Anew." *All the World's a Stage.* Charlottesville, VA: Walsch, 2001. Print.

Endnotes

1. Gordon, Wendy. "American Cities Get Smart about Energy | Smarter Cities." *Main | Smarter Cities*. Natural Resources Defense Council, 19 July 2010. Web. 08 Feb. 2011. <http://smartercities.nrdc.org/articles/american-cities-get-smart-about-energy>.

2. Weaver, Dennis. "Ecolonomics . . . Think Anew, Act Anew." *All the World's a Stage*. Charlottesville, VA: Walsch, 2001. Print.

3. "Electricity FAQs - Energy Information Administration." *Independent Statistics and Analysis: U.S. Energy Information Administration*. U.S. Deptment of Energy, 29 Mar. 2010. Web. 11 Feb. 2011. <http://tonto.eia.doe.gov/ask/electricity_faqs.asp#electricity_use_home>.

4. "US Indoor Water Use | WaterSense | US EPA." *US Environmental Protection Agency*. 14 Dec. 2010. Web. 06 Feb. 2011. <http://www.epa.gov/watersense/pubs/indoor.html>.

5. "Progress and Results: City of Fort Collins." *City of Fort Collins, Colorado Official Website*. Web. 06 Feb. 2011. <http://www.fcgov.com/climatewise/progress.php>.

6. *FortZED*. Web. 11 Feb. 2011. <http://fortzed.com/>.

7. "Utilities: City of Fort Collins." *City of Fort Collins, Colorado Official Website*. 2011. Web. 14 Feb. 2011. <http://www.fcgov.com/utilities/business/rates/electric/coincident-peak>.

8. "Summary of RCRA | Laws & Regulations| US EPA." *US Environmental Protection Agency*. 13 Jan. 2011. Web. 11 Feb. 2011. <http://www.epa.gov/lawsregs/laws/rcra.html>.

9. Pirog, Rick, Timothy Van Pelt, Kamyar Enshayan, and Ellen Cook. "Leopold Center - Food, Fuel, and Freeways." Thesis. Leopold Center for Sustainable Agriculture, 2001. *Leopold*

Center for Sustainable Agriculture. June 2001. Web. 11 Feb. 2011. <http://www.leopold.iastate.edu/pubs/staff/ppp/>.

10. "Fish Consumption Advisories for the State of Colorado." *Colorado Department of Public Health and Environment.* Web. 11 Feb. 2011. <http://www.cdphe.state. co.us/wq/FishCon/faqs.html>.

11. "Population Estimates." *Census Bureau Home Page.* Population Division. Web. 11 Feb. 2011. <http://www.census.gov/popest/ archives/>.

12. "US Indoor Water Use | WaterSense | US EPA." *US Environmental Protection Agency.* Office of Waste Water Management. Web. 11 Feb. 2011. <http://www.epa.gov/ WaterSense/pubs/indoor.html>.

13. United States. General Accounting Office. *Freshwater Supply States' Views of How Federal Agencies Could Help Them Meet the Challenges of Expected Shortages : Report to Congressional Requesters.* [Washington, D.C.]: U.S. General Accounting Office, 2003. Print.

14. "Water To Waste Resource Information Section Two: Water Energy Efficiency Information and EPA WaterSense Program." *WasteWater Education.* Web. 11 Feb. 2011. <http:// www.wastewatereducation.org/w2w08/w2w08a.html>.

15. "Water To Waste Resource Information Section Two: Water Energy Efficiency Information and EPA WaterSense Program." *WasteWater Education.* Web. 11 Feb. 2011. <http:// www.wastewatereducation.org/w2w08/w2w08a.html>.

16. "Water To Waste Resource Information Section Two: Water Energy Efficiency Information and EPA WaterSense Program." *WasteWater Education.* Web. 11 Feb. 2011. <http:// www.wastewatereducation.org/w2w08/w2w08a.html>.

17. "Complying with the Environmental Marketing Guides." *BCP Business Center.* Federal Trade Commission, May 2000. Web. 11 Feb. 2011. <http://business.ftc.gov/documents/bus42- complying-environmental-marketing-guides>.

18. "FAQs | The Sins of Greenwashing: Home and Family Edition." *The Sins of Greenwashing: Home and Family Edition.* TerraChoice Group Inc, 2011. Web. 11 Feb. 2011. <http:// sinsofgreenwashing.org/findings/faqs/>.

19. "Integrated Pest Management (IPM) Principles | Fact Sheets | About Pesticides | Pesticides | US EPA." *Pesticides: Topical & Chemical Fact Sheets.* US Environmental Protection Agency, 8 Dec. 2010. Web. 11 Feb. 2011. <http://www.epa.gov/opp00001/factsheets/ipm.htm>.

20. "Be Hydro-Logical | Drinking Water | US EPA." *Index | Water | US EPA.* United States Environmental Protection Agency, 21 Apr. 2010. Web. 11 Feb. 2011. <http://water.epa.gov/learn/kids/drinkingwater/behyrdological.cfm>.

21. "Water Conservation." *NCWCD Home Page.* The Northern Colorado Water Conservancy District. Web. 12 Feb. 2011. <http://www.ncwcd.org/ncwcd_about/water.asp>.

22. Ries, Al, and Jack Trout. *The 22 Immutable Laws of Marketing: Violate Them at Your Own Risk.* New York, NY: HarperBusiness, 1993. Print.

23. "accounting." *Collins English Dictionary | Complete & Unabridged 10th Edition.* HarpersCollins Publishers. Web. 14 Feb. 2011. <Dictionary.comhttp://dictionary.reference.com/browse/accounting>.

24. "The Triple Bottom Line | Strategies & Tools." *Business and Sustainable Development: A Global Guide.* International Institute for Sustainable Development (IISD), 17 Jan. 2000. Web. 16 Feb. 2011. <http://www.iisd.org/business/tools/principles_triple.asp>.

www.ingramcontent.com/pod-product-compliance
Lightning Source LLC
Chambersburg PA
CBHW022009170526
45157CB00003B/1207